Collins

NICHOLSON

WATERWAYS OF THE

Norfolk Broads

CONTENTS

Published by Nicholson
An imprint of HarperCollins Publishers
Westerhill Road, Bishopbriggs, Glasgow G64 2QT
www.harpercollins.co.uk

HarperCollins Publishers, Macken House,
39/40 Mayor Street Upper, Dublin 1, D01 C9W8, Ireland

First published by Nicholson 2010
New edition published 2012, 2014, 2018, 2022

© HarperCollins Publishers Ltd 2022

Researched and edited by Jonathan Mosse and
Cicely Oliver.

All photographs © Jonathan Mosse
(except page 94 © Shutterstock.com/yackers1)

Printed in Malaysia

ISBN 978-0-00-849069-0

10 9 8 7 6 5 4 3

MIX
Paper
FSC™ C007454

A catalogue record is available from the British Library.

This product uses map data licensed from Ordnance
Survey © Crown copyright and database rights (2021)
Ordnance Survey (100018598).

The representation in this publication of a road, track or
path is no evidence of the existence of a right of way.

The publishers greatly acknowledge the assistance given
by CAMRA representatives and branch members.

All rights reserved. No part of this publication may be
reproduced, stored in a retrieval system, or transmitted,
in any form or by any means, electronic, mechanical,
photocopying, recording or otherwise without the prior
permission in writing of the publisher and copyright owners.

Every care has been taken in the preparation of this
guide. However, the Publisher accepts no responsibility
whatsoever for any loss, damage, injury or inconvenience
sustained or caused as a result of using this guide.

HarperCollins does not warrant that any website mentioned
in this title will be provided uninterrupted, that any website
will be error free, that defects will be corrected, or that the
website or the server that makes it available are free of
viruses or bugs. For full terms and conditions please refer
to the site terms provided on the website.

INTRODUCTION

The Broads (the Norfolk and Suffolk Broads) are one of Britain's best-known holiday boating areas. They make up Britain's largest and most important protected wetland and are a national park providing a home to some of the rarest plants and animals in the country. A unique and enchanting wetland, with over 200 km (125 miles) of lock-free, navigable tidal waters, all waiting to be explored.

The area extends over the lower reaches of the Rivers Waveney, Yare and Bure, together with the Rivers Ant and Thurne (tributaries of the Bure) and the River Chet (the tributary of the Yare). The low-lying, wetland landscape contains around 60 shallow lakes. These lakes are referred to as 'broads', while we use the term 'the Broads' to refer to the entire area.

The history of the familiar landscape we see today dates back to the Middle Ages in the form of written evidence of peat digging in the Broads. By this time, much of the area had been cleared of woodland for fuel and building material. In the 12th century peat digging had become a major industry, the cut turfs being used for fuel. Almost every Broads settlement had its own pit, from where the peat was extracted on a huge scale. Gradually sea levels rose and the pits flooded making cutting more difficult until, by the 14th century, the peat diggings were abandoned.

For a long time, the origins of the broads were not properly understood. In 1952 Dr J M Lambert advanced the theory that these waterways were, in fact, man-made: a suggestion received with scepticism. However, researchers discovered that the sides of the broads were vertical, not gently sloping as would be the case with a naturally formed lake: evidence that these immense areas of water had originally been dug by hand. This was supported by the knowledge that there had been a massive demand for peat in the area, which by the 14th century was both densely populated and prosperous.

Historically, the Broads' economy was centred on agriculture and the profitable wool trade. The marshman's way of life exploited the natural landscape of the lowland river valleys by tending cattle, cutting reeds, building dykes and drainage mills, harvesting fish and hunting wildfowl.

In the 16th century, Norwich, after London, was the second largest city in England, its wealth built on wool, weaving, fishing, agriculture and general trade. There was a large export market from Norwich via Great Yarmouth and the waterways – natural and man-made – were major trading routes essential for communication and commerce, not only for meeting the large market for goods outside the area but for local communication supplying the riverside settlements.

The distinctive Norfolk wherries (see page 94 for a brief description) were developed to navigate this area of rivers and lakes, and for several hundred years provided essential transport. The coming of the railways in the 1870s started the decline in commercial sailing, as the area's transport system was developed and cargo-carrying was transferred to the trains. However, the railways also opened up the Broads to recreation and enterprising wherry owners converted their vessels to accommodate passengers in order to make up lost income. Inhabitants of the Broads had always used the waterways for pleasure, alongside their day-to-day work and these early wherry conversions were the start of the tourism business that has continued to expand over the years and now sees around seven million visitors enjoying the Broads annually.

However, the ensuing decades of increasing visitor numbers, boating and intensive agriculture had a detrimental effect on the fragile environment of this area. By the 1950s the clear Broads water had become cloudy and polluted, the river banks were eroding and the unmanaged fenland was turning into scrub. After alarming reports on the degradation of the Broads, the original Broads Authority was created in 1978 to manage the area. Following considerable success in dealing with the environmental problems and tackling restoration, the 1988 Broads Act gave status equivalent to a National Park, operating from 1989, one of 15 specially protected areas within the UK. The Broads National Park has three main aims: to conserve and enhance the natural beauty, wildlife and cultural heritage of the Broads; to promote opportunities for the understanding and enjoyment of the special qualities of the Broads by the public; to protect the interests of navigation. The National Park must have responsibility for the needs of agriculture and forestry and the economic and social interests of those who live or work in the Broads.

This guide is designed to help visitors plan their visit to the Broads in advance and to be a practical reference while exploring the area. For many people, the best way to discover the Broads is by boat and this book describes the varied ways in which you can get onto the water in all types of craft, whether for an hour's boat trip, for a week-long boating holiday, a day's canoeing or simply by hiring a rowing boat. Of course, not everyone wants to take to the water so we have also included lots of information for the casual visitor as well as those wishing to explore the area on foot or by bicycle, or to enjoy a day's fishing. There is also information listing places to eat and drink, together with places to visit. Unique features of the Broads are highlighted along with detailed descriptions of their formation. Find out how the Broads' traditional trading vessel – the wherry – has evolved, and how to enjoy their unfolding beauty from the serenity of a sailing boat.

Ted Ellis, one of Norfolk's best-loved naturalists and broadcasters, described the Broads as 'a breathing space for the cure of souls'. We hope that this guidebook will encourage you to explore the Broads, enjoy their unique atmosphere and special qualities, and to find your own breathing space.

If you would like to comment on any aspect of the guide, please write to Nicholson Waterways Guides, HarperCollins Publishers, Westerhill Road, Bishopbriggs, Glasgow G64 2QT or email nicholson@harpercollins.co.uk.

Also available:

Collins NICHOLSON

Waterways guides and map

1 **Grand Union, Oxford & the South East**

2 **Severn, Avon & Birmingham**

3 **Birmingham & the Heart of England**

4 **Four Counties & the Welsh Canals**

5 **North West & the Pennines**

6 **Nottingham, York & the North East**

7 **River Thames & the Southern Waterways**

Inland Waterways Map of Great Britain

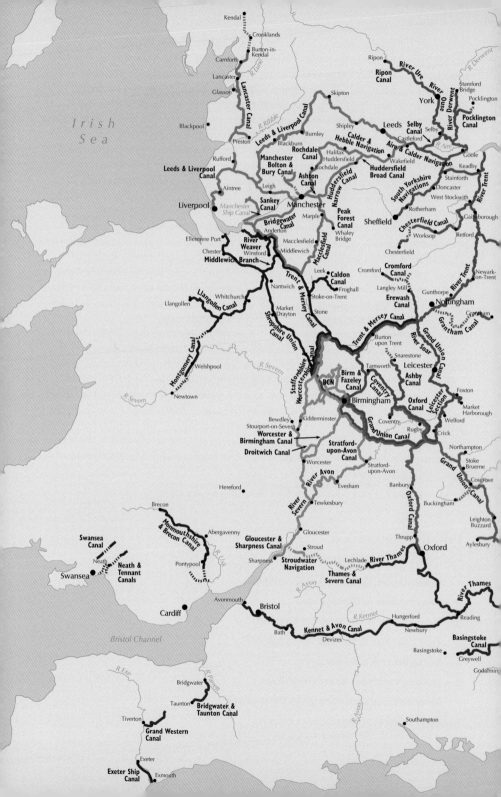

The Waterways of Britain

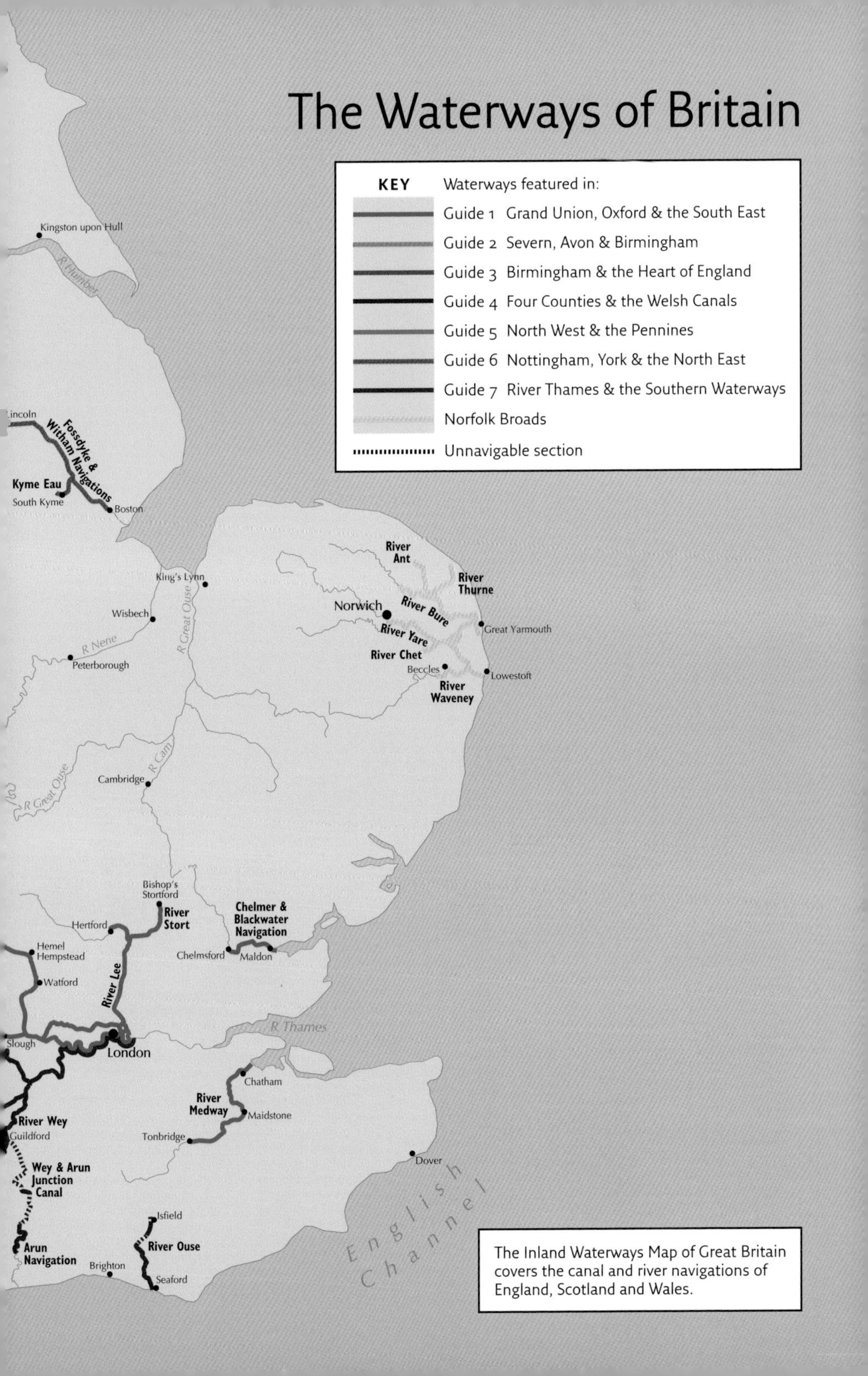

KEY   Waterways featured in:

Guide 1 Grand Union, Oxford & the South East

Guide 2 Severn, Avon & Birmingham

Guide 3 Birmingham & the Heart of England

Guide 4 Four Counties & the Welsh Canals

Guide 5 North West & the Pennines

Guide 6 Nottingham, York & the North East

Guide 7 River Thames & the Southern Waterways

Norfolk Broads

················· Unnavigable section

Kingston upon Hull

R Humber

Lincoln

Fossdyke & Witham Navigations

Kyme Eau

South Kyme

Boston

King's Lynn

Wisbech

R Nene

Peterborough

R Great Ouse

R Great Ouse

R Cam

Cambridge

River Ant

River Thurne

River Bure

Norwich

River Yare

Great Yarmouth

River Chet

Beccles

Lowestoft

River Waveney

Bishop's Stortford

River Stort

Chelmer & Blackwater Navigation

Hertford

Chelmsford

Maldon

Hemel Hempstead

River Lee

Watford

Slough

London

R Thames

Chatham

River Medway

Maidstone

Dover

River Wey

Guildford

Tonbridge

Wey & Arun Junction Canal

Isfield

Arun Navigation

Brighton

River Ouse

Seaford

English Channel

The Inland Waterways Map of Great Britain covers the canal and river navigations of England, Scotland and Wales.

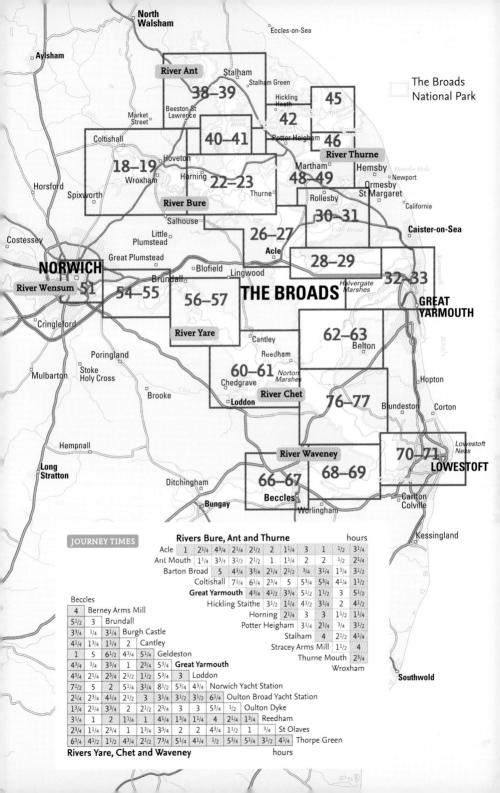

GENERAL INFORMATION FOR BROADS USERS

INTRODUCTION

The Norfolk and Suffolk Broads is Britain's largest protected wetland and third largest inland waterway, having the status of a National Park. It is also home to some of the rarest plants and animals in the UK. The Broads Authority was set up in 1989 with responsibility for conservation, planning, recreation and waterways and they can be contacted at Yare House, 62-64 Thorpe Road, Norwich NR1 1RY (01603 610734; www.broads-authority.gov.uk).

The Broads Authority has produced a series of helpful leaflets covering the Waterways Code for Broads users which can be found at https://www.broads-authority.gov.uk/boating/navigating-the-broads/safety/waterways-codes. These are supported by a suite of equally informative videos available at https://www.broads-authority.gov.uk/boating/navigating-the-broads/boating-essentials.

The Boater's Handbook is a 'booklet', now available in video form, produced jointly by the Canal & River Trust and the Environment Agency which contains an introduction to basic boat handling and safety information. It can be viewed at https://canalrivertrust.org.uk/enjoy-the-waterways/boating/a-guide-to-boating/boaters-handbook.

The sheer popularity of the Broads means that the navigation can be very busy throughout the season, which brings its own hazards and challenges. Having an understanding of this, and an insight into how to deal with the many situations that can arise, is your best way of staying safe and having an enjoyable holiday in one of Britain's most ecologically rich environments.

ACCIDENTS

If someone is injured or there is serious damage to your boat, or to someone else's, you must stop as soon as is practicable. Call 999 and ask for the coastguard.

- You must inform Broads Control of the incident (01603 756056) and give the name and address of the boat owner, and the boat registration number.
- You must also give this information to anyone else who has good reason to request it.
- Hire boaters must also inform their hire centre and there will be instructions on what to do in the *Skipper's Guide*.
- If you have an accident where property is damaged but no one is injured, you must stop your boat and give your name and address, that of the boat owner and the boat registration number, to anyone who has good reason to need it.
- You should take all reasonable steps to find out who the damaged property or boat belongs to, let them know in writing what has happened and give your name and address.
- Report incidents to Broads Control either by telephone 01603 756056, email *broads.control@broads-authority.gov.uk* via the Broads Authority web site.
- You may be liable to a fine of up to £1,000 if you do not follow these procedures.

BRIDGES

Bridges can be fixed or moveable. Bridge heights shown on the maps are for central clearance at high water on a normal tide. River levels vary considerably, depending upon weather conditions and the tide, and can affect the figures given.

- There is a gauge board on either side of the approach to most bridges, which will give you the current clearance available. Check this carefully to ensure that you have clearance.
- The air draft is the height of your boat from the waterline to the highest part of the boat (shown on a plate in the cockpit of hire boats).
- Think ahead when approaching all bridges. Lower the canopy and/or windscreen. Get everyone off the deck. Ensure that all hands and heads are in board in plenty of time before the bridge.
- Never race for a bridge or try to hurry through. Consider moored boats and monitor your boat wash. Keep to the speed limits.
- Watch for other boats coming through. Generally the boat travelling with the current has right of way.
- Don't raise your head until you are well clear of the bridge and **never** try to fend off using hands or feet.
- Yachts will need to lower their masts at all bridges except Reedham, Somerleyton and Trowse swing bridges and the lifting bridges on Breydon Water, and Novi Sad and Carrow Road bridges in Norwich.
- At Potter Heigham hire boats must use the bridge pilot from Phoenix Fleet boatyard to take you through, available *08.30-18.00*, depending on tide and weather conditions. Telephone *01692 670460*.

- At Wroxham there is an optional bridge pilot available to help you. Some hire boatyards insist that their customers use the service – check with the boatyard or look in the *Skipper's Manual*. The service is available 09.00–17.00. Telephone *07775 297638*.
- If you have any problems, telephone Broads Control on *01603 756056*. The tidal range is such that passage in one direction does not guarantee a return passage at all times. Check with pilots before proceeding.

Moveable bridges
- At lift and swing bridges, a single red flag indicates the bridge is working and in service; two red flags indicate that the bridge is not working and not in service.
- Bridges will only open for craft clearly unable to pass under (i.e. if you need to lower a canopy or windscreen, you must do so).
- The signal requiring the bridge to open is three prolonged blasts on the horn or whistle.
- Most bridges monitor *VHF channel 12*. The radio will not be answered during emergency matters relating to the rail network.
- The bridge operator will update electronic signage on the bridge to reflect waiting time before the bridge opens.
www.broads-authority.gov.uk/boating/navigating-the-broads/bridge-heights-and-opening-times

BOAT HANDLING
If you are hiring a boat, your boatyard will brief you thoroughly on the various controls, boat handling and manoeuvring, and mooring. You will also be provided with a *Skipper's Guide* for ready reference while you are onboard.
- A cruiser is big and heavy and has no brakes. To stop it you must put it into reverse – it can take a long time to stop, so you must think and plan ahead.
- The water in a river or broad is always moving. The water and your boat will be affected by the winds and tides. Be aware that steering straight may not keep you on a straight path.
- Steering a boat with a rudder is different from steering a car. The boat pivots on its centre point and it is the bow (front) and the stern (back) of the boat that move. You will be facing the bow, but always think about what the back end of your boat is doing, to prevent it swinging out into other boats or the bank.

- Always manoeuvre the boat at slow speeds. You must be able to operate your boat without causing injury to people, wildlife, the environment, moorings, structures on the banks and other property.
- In general children under eight must not drive a motor boat. There are some circumstances in which children aged between eight and fourteen may drive a motor boat – visit *www.broads-authority.gov.uk* and check the Navigation Byelaws for details.
- Most boats turn better in one direction than another. When viewed from behind, most boats' propellers turn clockwise – these boats will turn better to port (left).

BOAT SAFETY SCHEME
The Broads Authority operates the Boat Safety Scheme (BSS). This comprises essential safety requirements and *The Boat Safety Scheme Essential Guide* is available from the Broads Authority main office or direct from Boat safety Scheme, First Floor North, Station House, 500 Elder Gate, Milton Keynes MK9 1BB (0333 202 1000; www.boatsafetyscheme.org).

BOATYARDS
Boatyards and other facilities are shown on the maps with their details in the tables on pages 80–87. Hire boaters should always contact their hire centre with any queries in the first instance.

BROADS AUTHORITY RANGERS
The Rangers travel the Broads waterways in easily recognised boats. They enforce speed limits, carry out radar speed checks, and ensure that boats navigate properly. In addition, they are able to assist boaters with day-to-day issues including safety procedures, tidal conditions and planning.

BROADS CONTROL
Broads Control deals with everything to do with navigating the Broads and rivers, from routine enquiries to emergency liaison with the coastguard, police and the Environment Agency. During peak season the office gets busy, so please be patient and do use the answerphone provided. In the event of an emergency, dial *999* – the emergency services will always contact Broads Control as required. Contact Broads Control on *01603 756056* or email *broads.control@broads-authority.gov.uk*.

ELECTRIC CHARGING POINTS

There are electric charging points at 20 locations throughout the Broads, on the rivers Ant, Bure, Chet, Thurne, Waveney, Wensum and Yare. They are indicated on the relevant mapping pages or by visiting *www.broads-authority.gov.uk/boating/facilities*. The charging points not only enable electric boats to reliably travel throughout the Broads waterways, but allow the electricity supply on diesel powered boats to be topped up easily. The charging pillars are straight forward to use and the charging cards are available from the Broads Authority head office, Broads Information Centres and other outlets close to the charging points.

EMERGENCIES

- Contact the emergency services by calling *999* for coastguard, fire, police or ambulance services. To contact the police on less urgent matters dial *101*.
- On a hire boat, contact details for your boatyard will be in your *Skipper's Handbook*.
- If you have to contact the emergency services or your boatyard, be as specific as possible about your location. Use the nearest Broads Authority 24 hour mooring as a reference to where you are – the name of the mooring is shown on the signs. Always try to keep track of where you are on the Broads.
- Keep your mobile phone charged.
- Never enter the water, even in an emergency. Reach or throw but don't go into the water – reach with a broom, mop or towel, or throw a rope (keeping hold of one end), or anything that floats such as a life ring, ball or airtight container.

ENVIRONMENTALLY FRIENDLY BOATING

The Broads area is one of Europe's most important wetlands and conserving this beautiful but fragile environment is one of the responsibilities of the Broads Authority. As part of their work in sustainable tourism (recreation that does no lasting damage to the environment, or to people's enjoyment of it) the Authority actively promotes environmentally friendly boating.

- It is illegal to discharge sewage into the water of the Broads. Anyone doing so may be liable to a fine of up to £2,500. Facilities for pump out and sewage disposal are shown on the relevant map pages.
- Take extra care not to spill diesel into the water when refuelling. Spills of chemicals such as diesel cause harm to wildlife and can kill many water creatures. Spilling diesel or oil is a prosecutable offence.
- If you suspect an oil leak, do not pump out the bilges and release oil into the water. Instead, contact your boatyard immediately.
- If you see a pollution incident of any sort, telephone the Environment Agency on *01733 371811* or the Hotline *0800 80 70 60*
- If you have your own boat, consider electric power. It is clean and convenient and there are charging points around the Broads *(see Electric Charging Points)*. These charging points can also be used to charge on-board batteries: all you need is a cable with an appropriate socket to connect.
- All waste from boats, except sewage, empties straight into the river so that the cleaning products used have a direct impact on the environment. Reduce pollution by using biodegradable washing-up liquid and cleaning products, and try to use detergents containing no phosphate (also called sodium tripolyphosphate/STPP) or less then 5 per cent. Use only small amounts.
- Do not put cooking oil straight down the sink: absorb oil on to kitchen paper and put the paper in a bin. Oil can cause slicks on the water, causing particular problems for birds.
- Be careful with your rubbish. Discarded litter and fishing tackle can entangle and kill wildlife. Dispose of your rubbish carefully at proper sites. Do not leave bags of rubbish beside the bins, even if they are full – try to hold on to rubbish until you reach the next site.
- Facilities for recycling and waste disposal are often available near moorings or in the local town or village. Details can be obtained from Broads Information Centres.
- Noise pollution should be avoided too. Be sensitive to your neighbours when moored up. Do not leave your engine idling late at night or early in the morning. Also be aware of the volume of your radio or television, particularly when the roof of your boat is down. Causing a noise nuisance could result in a fine of up to £1,000.
- If you have a dog with you, please clear up after it. Remember that although dogs are allowed on public rights of way, under close control, many nature reserves do not allow access for dogs.
- Keep an eye out for the killer shrimp. Broads users are being urged to **Check, Clean** and **Dry** their boats and fishing equipment, before they enter the water, to help protect the waterways from the invasive killer shrimp. *Dikerogammarus villosus* is an

aggressive hunter, feeding on damselflies, small fish, water boatmen and native freshwater shrimp, threatening the Broads eco-system.

- Also be on the lookout for floating pennywort. It was sold in this country as an ornamental plant for garden ponds, but it has escaped into the wild, where it stops native plants from growing and can cause serious problems for flood control and navigation. Do not let garden water plants get into the rivers and broads. If you think you have seen floating pennywort in the wild, please contact the Broads Authority or the Environment Agency.
- The Upper Thurne Broads (Hickling, Horsey and Martham) are internationally important for water birds. If you are there during the winter, please avoid the refuge areas (marked by buoys). Large flocks of ducks and geese spend the winter on the open water where they feed and roost and the refuges allow them to stay undisturbed.
- The Green Blue is an environmental awareness initiative supported by the British Marine Federation and the Royal Yachting Association, for those in the marine business and all those who enjoy boating and watersports. Visit *www.thegreenblue.org.uk* or telephone *023 8060 4227* for lots of advice and information.

FUEL

Hire craft usually carry fuel sufficient for the rental period. Many boatyards will include the cost of fuel in the hire price. If you are charged, it will only be for the fuel used, and this will be deducted from your fuel deposit when you return the boat. The *Skipper's Notes* will include more details. If a garage is marked in the text for a town or village, it signifies that fuel is available there.

GOING AGROUND

The Broads is an area of tidal waterways and the tidal effect will be most strongly felt in the Breydon Water area and the lower reaches of the southern rivers. Water levels rise and fall depending upon the state of the tide. It is important to always stay within any channel marking posts. Should you go aground, try reversing gently, or pushing off with the boat hook or quant in the case of yachts. Another method is to get your crew to rock the boat from side to side using the boat hook, or move all crew to the end opposite to that which is aground. If you have any problems, contact your boatyard or telephone Broads Control on *01603 756056*.

LAVATORIES

Hire craft are usually fitted with flushing, sealed unit toilets. They are emptied via a process called 'pump out', which is simple and clean and carried out at boatyards and yacht stations. Pump out facilities are shown on the map pages. Have the toilets pumped out before things become critical. If you are hiring your craft, check the *Skipper's Notes* for more information.

LIFE-JACKETS

It is advisable to wear a life-jacket on deck at all times, even if you can swim. Children, the less mobile, and the elderly should always wear a life-jacket, even when the boat is moored. The water is very cold at all times of the year, and even strong swimmers can get into trouble quickly and tides and currents also need to be considered.

MOORING

Free moorings are available at many locations in the Broads for a maximum stay of 24 hours. These moorings can be used by all boats, and many of them can also be used by anglers. There are also moorings available at public staithes, pubs and boatyards, although there may be a charge to use these.

Mooring up and casting off can be one of the most difficult parts of handling a boat, but with preparation and a little practice you will soon be confident. Plan ahead – make sure that your ropes are ready and that your crew knows what to do. The fittest adult (not a child) should always step (not jump!) ashore and should wear a life-jacket.

- If the mooring is staffed, please follow all directions given by the rangers.
- Always approach a mooring against the tide, with a careful hand on the throttle. You will be able to to hold the boat stationary heading into the tide and approach the mooring sideways under control.
- Always drop your mud weight when moored, especially if mooring stern on (the back of the boat), when the mud weight will stop the bow (the front) swinging around.
- Allow slack in mooring ropes to allow for rises and falls in the water level as the tides rise and fall – check your mooring ropes regularly.
- Do not trail mooring ropes across footpaths and never run alongside moorings, to avoid tripping on ropes or posts.

NAVIGATION ADVICE

Ask any ranger, or telephone Broads Control on *01603 756056*. The Broads Authority publish *Waterways Code* leaflets covering such subjects as safety and mooring. The leaflets are available from the Authority and their Information Centres, and can also be downloaded from *www.broads-authority.gov. uk/boating/navigating-the-broads.*

REGATTAS

Regattas, organised by sailing, power boat and rowing clubs, are very much part of the boating heritage of the Broads. They can be great fun for spectators as well as the participants – bridges are often a good vantage point. Regular events take place each year and details are available from the Broads Information Centres and the Norfolk and Suffolk Boating Association (*www. thegreenbook.org.uk).* If you find yourself on the water during a regatta:

- Keep close to the right hand bank.
- Sailing boats have right of way. Slow down and try to pass behind them.
- Make your course clear – do not weave about.
- Watch for any indications by the crew as to when they would like you to pass, but do not put yourself or others in danger.
- In some areas particular channels may be provided for your safe passage. In these cases stay within the channel. During powerboat racing, do not enter or leave via the body of the broad where the event is taking place.
- Listen carefully to any advice, and follow any guidance from navigation rangers or safety patrol boats.

RULES OF THE ROAD

- Keep your boat close to the right hand bank.
- Sailing boats have right of way over motor boats. Slow down and try to pass behind them.
- Make your course clear – do not weave about or try to stop suddenly.
- Watch for any indications by other crews as to when they would like you to pass, but do not put yourself or others in danger.
- In some areas particular channels may be provided for your safe passage. In these cases, stay within the channel. During powerboat racing, do not enter or leave via the body of the broad where the racing is taking place.
- Listen carefully to, and take any guidance from navigation rangers or safety patrol boats.
- Keep clear of commercial traffic and watch for any instructions from their crew.
- Keep clear of craft under tow.

- Do not exceed the speed limits.
- Navigation lights are required after dark. (Generally, hire boats may not travel after dark.)
- You must not fish from a motor or sailing boat which is underway.

SLIPWAYS AND LAUNCH SITES

There are public slipways at Beccles (page 67; 01502 712225), Hickling Staithe (page 42), Horning (page 22; 01692 630434), Horstead (page 70), Hoveton Riverside Park (page 19), Oulton Broad Yacht Station (01502 574946) and the Water Sports Centre (01502 587163) both on page 70, Pug Lane Staithe at Repps with Bastwick (page 49), Smallburgh Staithe at Wayford Bridge (page 38), Sutton Staithe (page 39), Cantley (page 60) and South Walsham (page 26).

Some boatyards have slipways that can be used for a small charge and the Broads Authority publish a comprehensive list of all slipways at: www.broads-authority.gov.uk/ boating/facilities/slipways-and-launching-points.

SPEED LIMITS

There are speed limits of 3, 4, 5 or 6 mph in force throughout the Broads waterways. The limits are in place to reduce erosion of the river banks, prevent disturbance to water-level nesting birds, and protect people on moored boats. They are clearly signed on the riverbanks and are enforced by the navigation rangers. There is no need to go any faster – the faster you go, the bigger a wave (wash) the boat creates: if your wash is breaking against the bank, causing large waves or throwing moored boats around, slow down. Even if you are under the speed limit, you may still be fined if you are creating excess wash, so check it regularly, especially if you are on a day boat or just getting used to the speed of your boat at the start of a holiday. Slow down also when passing engineering works and anglers, when there is a lot of floating rubbish on the water (try to drift over obvious obstructions in neutral), when approaching blind corners, bridges and junctions. Remember that if your boat is moving in the same direction as the tide, your speed will be faster than indicated. The Broads Authority asks anyone who witnesses boats that are speeding or being driven carelessly to note details such as the boat name or registration, take photos or videos if they can, and report the incident to Broads Control on 01603 756056 or by email: Broads.Control@broads-authority.gov.uk.

TIDE TABLES

Tide tables are available from Broads Authority Information Centres and *www.broads-authority.gov.uk*. Local newspapers also publish tide times and the BBC website lists them, at *www.bbc.co.uk/weather/coast*.

TOLLS AND REGISTRATION

Any vessel kept or used within the Broads Authority navigational area for more than 28 days must be registered with the Authority, carry third party insurance and have paid the appropriate annual toll which can be paid through the Broads Authority main office.

URGENT BOATING INFORMATION

It is important that all skippers keep up to date with the latest available boating information available from the Broads Authority website. *www.broads-authority.gov.uk/boating/navigating-the-broads/urgent-boating-information*.

WATER

Hire boats will have a full tank of water for drinking and washing. You should top up your water regularly. Water points are indicated on the map pages. If you are hiring a boat, check the *Skipper's Notes* for more information.

WATER SKIING

Water skiing has been a regular Broads activity since 1951. Today there are 10 allocated ski zones on the rivers Waveney and Yare, together with a further zone on Breydon Water. Water skiing may only take place at certain times and all skiers must be members of the Eastern Rivers Water Ski Club and British Water Ski. More information, including the times water skiing is permitted, is available from the Easter Rivers Water Ski club website at *www.erwsc.co.uk*.

- Boat owners must obtain a skiing permit from the Broads Authority.
- All boat drivers must have passed the Sports Boat Drivers Award.
- All boats must have British Water Ski approved public liability insurance.
- Each of the water skiing zones on the Broads is clearly sign-posted. If you cruise through one of the water ski areas you must proceed cautiously as there may be skiers in the water.

- Keep to the right hand side of the river wherever possible.
- Keep a constant speed and course. Stop only to avoid collision or a skier in the water. Ski boats are fast and manoeuvrable and will keep out of your way.
- A yellow flag will be flown by all ski boats when skiing is underway. On seeing the flag, slow down, give the ski boat a wide berth and keep an extra look out for skiers in the water.

WEIL'S DISEASE

Weil's disease is a potentially serious, and even fatal condition, which can be contracted from rivers and other water sources, through cuts and scratches. Always wash your hands after contact with the water. If you fall in, wash yourself thoroughly, or shower, and wash your wet clothes before wearing them again. Clean cuts and scratches with an antiseptic and protect them with a plaster. The infection may seem like flu in the early stages and can occur two-four weeks after exposure. If you experience any flu-like symptoms after contact with the water, get medical advice immediately and mention the possibility of Weil's disease – not all medical practitioners will immediately consider it. More information is available from *www.leptospirosis.org*.

YACHT STATIONS

The Broads Authority run yacht stations at Norwich and Great Yarmouth offering a full range of facilities. They are staffed *daily 08.00-20.00 from Sat before Easter to first week Nov.* There is also a quay attendant at Reedham Quay *daily 09.00-18.00* for the same period. *(Norwich 01603 612980 Great Yarmouth 01493 842794 www.broads-authority.gov.uk/boating/facilities/yacht-stations)*. There are also Local Authority-run Yacht Stations situated at The Quay, Beccles NR34 9BH *(01502 712225/07938 845744; www.broadsnet.co.uk/beccles)* and Bridge Road, Lowestoft NR33 9JS *(01502 574946; www.yachtstation.co.uk/oulton-broad-moorings)*.

Wroxham

THE RIVER BURE

The Broads Authority publish guidance to the River Bure at www.broads-authority.gov.uk/boating/navigating-the-broads/water-depths/river-bure which includes further helpful tips and can be read in conjunction with this guide. For the River Ant, see www.broads-authority.gov.uk/boating/navigating-the-broads/water-depths/river-ant and, for the River Thurne, visit www.broads-authority.gov.uk/boating/navigating-the-broads/water-depths/river-thurne. These are particularly useful for water depth, speed limits and channel details which can alter regularly due to bank works and tidal movement.

Rising south of Melton Constable in Norfolk, the River Bure flows gently south east to Great Yarmouth. The Rivers Ant and Thurne join below Horning. In 1773 a bill was passed by Parliament to extent the existing navigation of 31 miles, which ended at Horstead Mill, up as far as Aylsham. Locks were built at Coltishall, Buxton Mill, Oxnead Mill, Burgh-near-Aylsham Mill and Aylsham, while the work was completed in October 1779. It was soon found that silting had occurred, reducing the depth to 3ft in places – in view of this regular dredging or 'didling' had to be carried out. Thirteen-ton wherries carried timber, coal, bricks (from Oxnead) agricultural produce, flour (from the mills) and marl from the Horstead Hall Estate.

The navigation prospered until the coming of the Wroxham to Aylsham railway in 1880 and the North Walsham to Melton Constable line in 1883 and survived until 1912, when severe flooding all the locks and funds for their repair could not be raised. Formal abandonment came in 1928. Today the river is once again navigable only as far as Horstead.

In 1825 work began on the North Walsham & Dilham Canal to extend navigation on the River Ant from Wayford Bridge to Antingham. John Millington was employed as the engineer and he cut a true canal (not an improved river navigation) through difficult, marshy land. The official opening took place in 1826 and when built, the canal was 8¾ miles long with six locks. The cargoes carried were typical of those of an agricultural area. As early as 1830 it became clear the canal would not be financially viable and in 1886 the company was forced to sell the navigation for £600. The initial share capital raised had been £29,300! Inevitably things went from bad to worse – the section above Swayfield Locks was abandoned in 1893 and damage was sustained in the 1912 floods. Ownership passed to the North Walsham Canal Company but in spite of improvements made below Swayfield Locks in the 1920s the end came in 1934, when the last wherry left the canal. Today only the short section to Tonnage Bridge remains navigable (smaller craft to Honing Common). The North Walsham Canal Company still exists and the navigation is now under restoration by the enthusiastic North Walsham & Dilham Canal Trust (07774 320068; www.nwdct.org). Today, one family and three companies own different sections of the canal.

WALKING AND CYCLING

The Wherryman's Way is a 35-mile long-distance path connecting Norwich with Great Yarmouth, exploring some of the most attractive stretches of the River Yare. There are 12 shorter walks, varying from one to seven miles, that can be picked up along the way. See www.herbertwoods.co.uk/norfolk-broads/walking/wherrymans-way for further details.

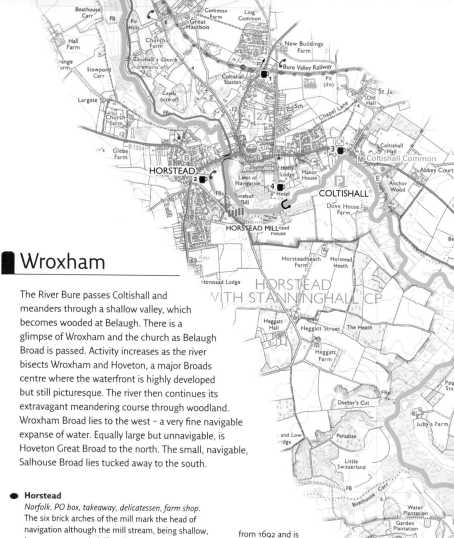

Wroxham

The River Bure passes Coltishall and meanders through a shallow valley, which becomes wooded at Belaugh. There is a glimpse of Wroxham and the church as Belaugh Broad is passed. Activity increases as the river bisects Wroxham and Hoveton, a major Broads centre where the waterfront is highly developed but still picturesque. The river then continues its extravagant meandering course through woodland. Wroxham Broad lies to the west – a very fine navigable expanse of water. Equally large but unnavigable, is Hoveton Great Broad lies to the north. The small, navigable, Salhouse Broad lies tucked away to the south.

● Horstead

Norfolk. PO box, takeaway, delicatessen, farm shop.
The six brick arches of the mill mark the head of navigation although the mill stream, being shallow, is not recommended. The village, which has some handsome houses, lies ½ mile to the north west. All Saints church, standing on rising ground by the river, has a slender 13th-C tower topped with a weather vane, and a 14th-C south door, although the rest of the church dates from 1879. There is some notable stained glass by Burne-Jones and Kempe.

● Coltishall

PO box, stores, off-licence, butcher, greengrocer, takeaways, garage. Half a mile from the moorings by the common. The church of St John the Baptist has a 12th-C chancel and a curious Victorian circular window on the north side. Facing the church along the main street is a rich selection of pretty 18th-C red-brick houses built at a time when Coltishall was more important than Wroxham. Note the flint-built school and The Limes, at the east end, which dates

from 1692 and is particularly handsome. Many of the best-known wherries were built in Allans Boatyard in Coltishall, they also built 'keels'– the forerunners of the Norfolk wherry. There is a fine antique and period glassworks in the village (www.antique-periodglassworks.co.uk).

Blickling Hall Blickling, Norwich NR11 6NF (01263 738030; www.nationaltrust.org.uk/blickling-estate). An important Jacobean mansion built 1616-27 for Sir Henry Hobart (Lord Chief Justice) by Robert Lyminge, who designed Hatfield House 12 years earlier. Red brick with stone dressings, the house stands in gardens surrounded by massive yew hedges. The interior is notable for the plasterwork ceiling in the great gallery and the state bedroom. The park is *open all year* and fishing permits are available for the

20-acre lake *Jun–Feb*. Restaurant, cafés, shop, bookshop, plant centre and cycle hire (including electric bikes and tagalongs). See website *for opening times* of the different elements of the estate.

- **Belaugh**
  Norfolk. PO box. A tiny village around the Norman church of St Peter which stands on a hill by the river. The cauldron-shaped font is made of blue stone while the tapestry-work hassocks were made locally.

- **Wroxham (and Hoveton)**
  Norfolk. *PO, stores, off-licence, chemists, takeaways, fish & chips, DIY, laundrette, library, garage, station.* Two villages divided by the river but colloquially lumped together as Wroxham – the major

Broads holiday centre, bustling with boats and boaters during the summer months. Before the coming of the railway (c1880) Wroxham was a tiny settlement around the church and the manor house, facing the river and open country to the west and even today still surprisingly intact. The mostly Perpendicular church of St Mary has a gloriously decorated Norman south door and many monuments, of which the one to Daniel Collyer (dated 1774) is outstanding – both pretty and graceful. The gabled manor house is to the south east of the church. St John's church, Hoveton, stands alone to the east. Its brick tower was built in 1765. Hoveton House (private) three quarters of a mile south east of the church, is a naïve red-brick building, considered one of the most attractive in Norfolk. There are many boatyards in the village offering craft for hire and the *weekends* can be busy as they are turned around for their new hirers. The stores are *open 07.30–22.00 (Sun 09.00–21.00)*.

The River Bure Wroxham

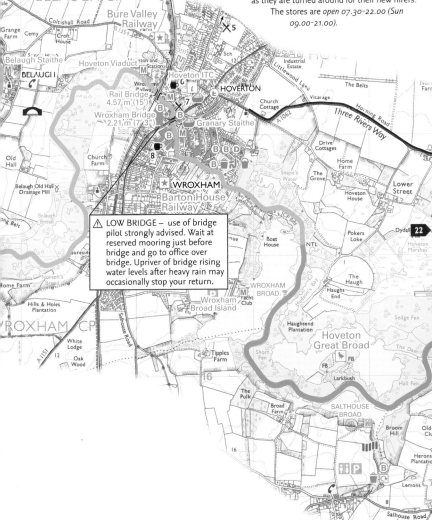

⚠ LOW BRIDGE – use of bridge pilot strongly advised. Wait at reserved mooring just before bridge and go to office over bridge. Upriver of bridge rising water levels after heavy rain may occasionally stop your return.

19

Barton House Railway Hartwell Road, The Avenue, Wroxham NR12 8TL (01603 782008; www.bartonhouserailway.org.uk). The golden age of steam railways is re-created at this site beside the River Bure, with two ride-on railways, authentic tickets and museum of railway artefacts. The signal box was originally built in 1901 at Honing Station and visitors can watch the signalman at work. Home baking and light meals. *Open Apr-Oct 3rd Sun in every month and Easter Mon 14.30-17.30.* Charge.

BeWILDerwood Horning Road, Hoveton NR12 8JW (01692 633033; www.bewilderwood.co.uk). A wild and imaginative adventure park for both children and grown ups, with tree houses, zip wires, jungle bridges, boat trips and marsh walks. It is the setting for the children's book *A Boggle at BeWilderwood*, by local author Tom Blofeld. Broadland Cycle Hire offers bike hire from the car park. Café. Picnic areas and plenty of outdoor seating. Disabled play equipment and facilities but upper woodland area is naturally sloping and may be difficult to access. Guide dogs only. *Open daily 10.00-17.00 or dusk if earlier, please check before visiting.* Charge.

Bure Valley Railway Aylsham Station, Norwich Road, Aylsham NR11 6BW (01263 733858; www.bvrw.co.uk). Narrow gauge railway running both steam and diesel locomotives between Aylsham and Wroxham, with connections to Broads trips at Wroxham (maximum of two dogs allowed per boat). The railway runs along the Bure valley footpath and cycleway and cycles can be carried aboard scheduled services. Restaurant and shop. Workshop visits. Everything wheelchair accessible. Well behaved dogs welcome. *Open Easter-Oct. Telephone or visit website for timetable information.* Charge.

Hoveton Great Broad Nature Trail (0845 600 3078; www.hovetongreatbroad.org.uk). Part of Bure Marshes. No access by road, reached by water from moorings on the River Bure beside the entrance. There is a marked trail through woodland on the edge of the broad.

Wroxam Barns Tunstead Road, Hoveton NR12 8QU (01603 783762; www.wroxhambarns.co.uk). Craft studios, plant centre, farmers' market, children's farm and funfair, all set in and around restored barns and agricultural buildings. Restaurant. Guide dogs only. *Open daily 10.00-17.00.* Admission free. Charge for children's farm and funfair (children under two go free).

Tourist Information Centre Station Road, Hoveton, Norwich NR12 8UR (01603 782281; www.broads-authority.gov.uk). The Centre is on the River Bure and has information and displays about Hoveton and the Broads. The Centre also offers a wildlife boat trip on Ra, a disabled-friendly solar boat that journeys along the River Bure towards Coltishall and back during the season, with plenty of time to enjoy the woodlands and meadows of this tranquil and varied stretch of river. *Open Apr-May & Oct Mon-Fri 09.00-13.00 and 13.30-17.00; Sat-Sun 09.00-17.00. Jun-Sep daily 09.00-17.00.*

● **Salhouse**

Norfolk. PO box, station (distant). South west of the navigation, this typical Broads village has two fine pubs somewhat scattered about. The church of all Saints dates partly from 12thC while incomplete later work has a curiously unfinished appearance.

A Busy Scene at Horning Ferry

WALKING AND CYCLING

Broadland Cycle Hire (07747 483154; www.norfolkbroadscycling.co.uk) offers bike hire from the car park at BeWilderwood (see page 20)

NAVIGATIONAL NOTES

1   The limit of navigation is at the entrance to the old lock cut below the arches of Horstead Mill, where it is possible to turn.
2   The air draught for Wroxham Bridge is 7' 6" at normal water levels.

BOAT TRIPS

Edwardian-style launch *Ra* offers trips up river from Hoveton to Coltishall *Apr-May & Oct weekends, 11.00, 12.00, 14.00 & 15.00 and Jun-Sep daily 11.00, 12.00, 14.00, 15.00 & 16.00.*
Richardson's The Rhond, Hoveton NR12 8UE (01603 782309; www.richardsonsboatingholidays. co.uk/norfolk-broads-day-boat-hire) offer electric and diesel day boat hire.
See also Tourist Information Centre above for trips aboard electric boat *Ra*.
Secret'SUP Paddle Boarding 4 Anchor Street, Coltishall, Norwich NR12 7AQ (07702 279680; www. secretsup.co.uk). Operating from a private garden on the banks of the River Bure in Coltishall, Secret'SUP provide lessons for beginners and novices and board hire for those with some paddling experience. *Weekdays only.*
The Canoe Man Wroxham 65 Bells Road, Gorleston NR31 6AG (07873 748408; www.thecanoeman. com/contact-us). A plethora of different trips available, offering a unique way to see the Broads. Telephone or visit website for further details.
Wroxham Launch Hire Kings Staithe, The Bridge, Wroxham NR12 8DA (01603 783143; wroxhamlaunchhire.co.uk). Day boat hire by the hour or the day.

Details of all the electric trip boats operated by the Broads Authority can be found at www.broads-authority.gov.uk/boating/hiring-a-boat/boat-trips.

Pubs and Restaurants (pages 18–19)

🍺✕ 1 **Jollys** North Walsham Road, Swanton Abbot NR10 5DW (01692 538863). Open-plan, but with different drinking areas, this rural pub serves real ale and *limited food (telephone for times)*. Beer garden, dogs welcome. *Regular* live music. Traditional pub games, newspapers, real fires and Wi-Fi. Camping. *Open Mon-Thu L and E & Fri-Sun 12.00-23.00 (Sun 22.30).*

🍺✕ 2 **The Recruiting Sergeant** Norwich Road, Horstead NR12 7EE (01603 737077; www. recruitingsergeant.co.uk). Large establishment, majoring on dining, serving food *Mon-Sat L and E & Sun 12.00-20.00*. Real ales. Garden, dog- and family-friendly. Wi-Fi. B&B. *Open 11.00-23.00 (Sun 12.00).*

🍺✕ 3 **The King's Head** Wroxham Road, Coltishall NR12 7EA (01603 737426; www. kingheadcoltishall.co.uk). A fine 17th-C hostelry, with Dutch gables, dispensing real ale and an excellent restaurant serving food *Mon-Sat L and E & Sun 12.00-23.00*. Garden and Wi-Fi. B&B. *Open Mon-Sat L and E & Sun 11.00-23.00.*

🍺✕ 4 **The Norfolk Restaurant at the Norfolk Mead Hotel** Church Lake, Coltishall NR12 7DN (01603 737531; www.norfolkmead.co.uk). Former Georgian merchant's house serving appetising meals sourced from fresh, local ingredients *L and E*, together with afternoon teas. B&B. Mooring.

✕🍷 5 **Wroxham Barns Restaurant Café** Tunstead Road, Hoveton NR12 8QU (01603 783762; www.wroxhambarns.co.uk). Home-cooked dishes and traditional teas with freshly-baked scones and cakes. *Open daily 10.00-17.00.*

🍺✕ 6 **The Kings Head Hotel** Station Road, Hoveton NR12 8UR (01603 782429; www. greenekinginns.co.uk/hotels/the-kings-head-hotel). Family-friendly, carvery-oriented pub serving real ale and food *daily 12.00-21.00*. Large riverside garden. *Open Mon-Sat 11.00-23.00 (Fri-Sat 00.00) & Sun 12.00-23.00.*

✕🍷 7 **The Old Mill Restaurant & Café Bar** The Bridge, 243 Norwich Road, Wroxham NR12 8DA (01603 783744; www.facebook.com/ TheOldMillCafeBar). Family-run restaurant which has been a part of the community for 40 years. Excellent coffee, cakes, meals and drinks. *Open Wed-Mon 09.00-16.00.*

🍺 8 **The Boat Shed** The Peninsular, Staitheway Road Wroxham NR12 8TH (01603 781952). Large single-room pub with a waterside terrace in the middle of a boatyard serving real ale and food *Mon-Sat L and E (not Mon L) and Sun 16.00-21.00.* garden. *Open Mon-Fri 17.00-23.00 & Sat-Sun 12.00-23.00.*

Horning

Typical carr woodland persists on each bank with the occasional small unnavigable broad just visible through the thick growth. Horning lies to the north after Hoveton Little Broad (*navigable summer only*) while outlying villas and chalets gradually give way to the more substantial but equally charming dwellings in the village. It's a busy place with plenty of boating activity, both hire boats and private craft. Then once again the woodland takes over, thinning on the north bank to allow a sight of Horning church. At Horning Hall the view at last widens and the River Ant joins from the north.

● **Woodbastwick**

Norfolk. An estate village of thatched cottages around a green. The church bears a dedication unique in the country, St Fabian and St Sebastion. Dating from 14th C, it was restored by Sir G. G. Scott in 1878-79. The tie beam roof is of interest. Ferry road leads down to the river and Cockshoot Broad to the north east where there is parking and a footpath leading to the Broad.

● **Horning**

Norfolk. PO, stores, off-licence, takeaways. A Broadland holiday centre but perhaps less commercially so than Wroxham. Thatched Edwardian lodges fronted by lawns together with thatched boathouses land a touch of elegance to the riverside with new, bijou, executive residences in between. The church of St Benedict stands separate from the village, a mile to the east.

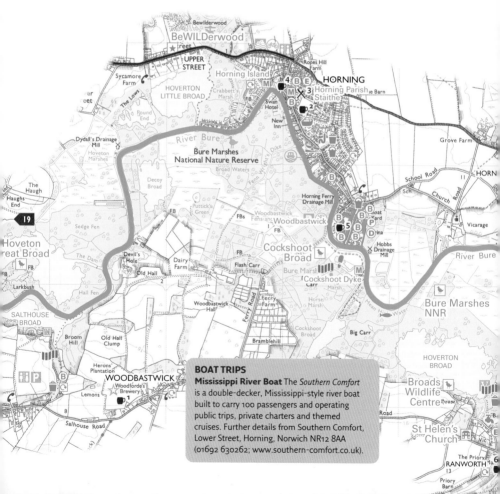

BOAT TRIPS

Mississippi River Boat The *Southern Comfort* is a double-decker, Mississippi-style river boat built to carry 100 passengers and operating public trips, private charters and themed cruises. Further details from Southern Comfort, Lower Street, Horning, Norwich NR12 8AA (01692 630262; www.southern-comfort.co.uk).

Dating from 13th C, its north aisle and porch were dismantled and sold off in the mid 18th C to pay for a new roof. Horning Hall (private) lies a further mile to the east – the barn (visible from the river) was once the Chapel of St James's Hospital, connected to St Benet's Abbey Gatehouse by a causeway. The remains of the Gatehouse, with an 18th-C windmill built onto it, is the most curious of all Broads landmarks. A regatta is held in Horning *each August* and the Three Rivers Race starts from here *in early June*. The ferry to Woodbastwick runs throughout the *summer months* and details are available from 07393 458682; www.horningfootferry.co.uk. There is an open-framed trestle wind pump standing on the east bank of the river known as Hobbs Mill.

● **Ranworth**
Norfolk. PO, stores, off-licence. The tall square tower of St Helen's church is visible for miles and those who climb to the top will be rewarded with magnificent views. The 15th-C rood screen, with its 12 delicately painted saints; dogs, ducks, swans and lions are considered the finest in Norfolk, The reredos of the two side altars also have painted figures. It was all discovered during the 19th C when whitewash was removed. The *Sarum Antiphoner* – a leather book brilliantly illuminated with burnished gold – was illustrated

by the monks of Langley Abbey in 1400 and written on sheep skin. Lost for 300 years, it was found in a private collection and subsequently sold to the church for 50 guineas.

Broadland Conservation Centre – Norfolk Wildlife Trust, Ranworth NR13 6HY (01603 270479; www.norfolkwildlifetrust.org.uk). A ½-mile nature trail which starts to the north of the church, leads through Ranworth Marshes to a thatched building floating on pontoons between Ranworth and Malthouse Broads. An exhibition shows the natural life of the Broads, emphasising the need for conservation. Gift shop and light refreshments. Centre *open Apr-Oct* and the reserve is *open all year, dawn to dusk.* No dogs. There is a boat service around the Broad. Charge.

Ranworth Information Centre Farm Lane, The Staithe, Ranworth NR13 6HY (01603 756094). The Visitor Centre is situated at picturesque Ranworth Staithe, overlooking Malthouse Broad. The Centre offers information and displays about the local area and the rest of the Broads National Park, as well as a selection of books, maps and gifts for sale. There is a boat trip on *Liana*, an Edwardian-style launch, which explores Malthouse Broad, Ranworth Dam and the nearby River Bure.

NAVIGATIONAL NOTES

1 Hoveton Little Broad – or Black Horse Broad – *is open for a week at Easter and from Whitsun to Oct.*
2 Horning sailing club have a busy *all year round* sailing calendar so boaters should be on the lookout for sailing dinghies at all times.

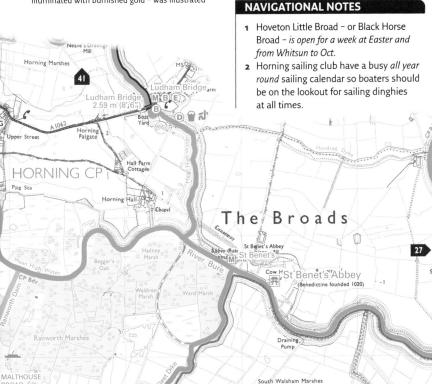

Pubs and Restaurants (pages 22-23)

🍺✕ **1 The Fur & Feather Inn** Slad Lane, Woodbastwick NR13 6HQ (01603 720003; www.thefurandfeather.co.uk). Housed in three old cottages, this welcoming hostelry is the Woodforde Brewery tap (and shop) serving a range of real ales from the adjoining brewery, together with excellent food *Mon-Sat L and E & Sun 12.00-18.00*. Family room and a large, pretty garden. Dog- and family-friendly. Wi-Fi. Mooring. *Open Mon-Fri 11.00-22.00 & Sat-Sun 10.00-23.00 (Sun 21.00)*.

🍺✕ **2 The New Inn** 54 Lower Street, Horning NR12 8PF (01692 631101; www.facebook.com/thenewinnhorning). Cask ales, cocktails and traditional, homemade, classic pub food served *L and E. Summer opening at 08.00* for breakfast. Waterside terrace with electric boat hook-up. Family-friendly. Wi-Fi. Mooring. *Open 11.00-23.00*.

✕🍷 **3 Bure River Cottage Restaurant** 27 Lower Street, Horning NR12 8AA (01692 631421; www.burerivercottagerestaurant.co.uk). Speciality seafood restaurant, mainly serving local fish and home-grown vegetables. Child-friendly. *Open Tue-Sat 17.30-21.00*.

🍺✕ **4 The Swan Inn** 10 Lower Street, Horning NR12 8AA (01692 630316; www.vintageinn.co.uk). Dating from 1897 and occupying a predominantly late-Victorian building, this pub offers real ale and food available *daily 12.00-22.00 (Sun 21.30)*. Waterside terrace. B&B. *Open 12.00-23.00 (Sun 22.30)*.

🍺 **5 TFI** Horning Ferry Road, Horning NR12 8PS (01692 630259; www.horningferry.co.uk). Selling a range of real ales, lagers and beers, the child-friendly menu includes a *daily* carvery available 12.00-21.00. Large waterside terrace in a popular area close to boatyards. Games room, real fires and Wi-Fi. *Open 12.00-23.00 (Sun 22.30)*.

🍺✕ **6 The Maltsters** The Hill, Ranworth NR13 6AB (01603 270900; www.facebook.com/themaltstersranworth). Large, comfortable pub just five minutes' walk from the Broads Wildlife Centre, dispensing real ale and food *daily L and E*. Large sheltered garden, dog- and child-friendly. Real fires, Newspapers and Wi-Fi. Camping nearby. *Open 11.00-22.30 (Sun 21.30)*.

Craft Old and New

Acle

Marshland now begins to predominate as the river passes what little remains of St Benet's Abbey, parts of the old walls showing clearly in the river bank. At Thurn Mouth the Bure makes a sharp turn south towards Acle and the distant windmills define the course ahead. There are posts marking a measured ¼ mile here and you can check your speed: multiply your time between the posts by 4 and divide the result by 60. If the answer is more than 7, slow down! Upton Dyke provides access to the village and the opportunity to examine a unique drainage mill. After passing the handsome Clippesby Mill, Acle Bridge is reached, attended by cruiser bases and *a pub*. The village is a mile away to the south west at this point and is best approached from the staithe further south. A flurry of boats marks the entrance to Acle Dyke before the reed-fringed river enters open country once again.

NAVIGATIONAL NOTES

1 If you are making the passage through Great Yarmouth and Breydon Water to the Southern Broads, you should arrive at the Yacht Station *within one hour after low water slack*. DO NOT attempt to make the passage at full ebb or flow – it is potentially dangerous. If in doubt as to whether it's safe to cross, call Broads Control (01603 756056) or Great Yarmouth Yacht Station (01493 842794).

2 You will also find this helpful: www.broads-authority.gov.uk/boating/navigating-the-broads/getting-safely-through-great-yarmouth.

● **St Benet's Abbey**
NR29 5NU (www.stbenetsabbey.org). There are but scant remains of this foundation, which may have existed even before it was endowed with three manors by King Canute (Cnut) in 1020. Overwhelmed by floodwater in 1287, most of the site was rebuilt – including the gatehouse and outer wall – and these defences were later tested in 1381 when the monastery was attacked by peasants. After the Dissolution the site was quarried for building materials, leaving only the gatehouse, joined to Horning Hall by a causeway, onto which the 18thC windmill has been built. There are also fragments of the church to be seen, together with a derelict 18th-C windmill. The last Abbot became Bishop of Norwich and a service is held here on the *first Sunday in August*, when the Bishop arrives by boat (usually a wherry) commemorates this fact.

● **South Walsham**
Norfolk. PO box. A pleasant village, south of the Broad, which has two churches sharing one churchyard, the result of an amalgamation of parishes just over a century ago. Until 1992 St Lawrence lay partly in ruins, having been burnt out in 1827, while St Mary survived and is an extremely handsome, mainly Perpendicular, building. The screen is notable and many of the pew ends are carved with poppy heads, some 600 years old. Now fully restored, the repurposed church of St Lawrence provides a unique centre for training and the arts. The walk by South Walsham Broad along Fleet Dyke to the river is excellent.

Fairhaven Woodland and Water Garden
School Road, South Walsham, Norwich NR13 6DZ (01603 270449; www.fairhavengarden.co.uk). 131 acres of ancient woodland, water gardens and a private broad, described as a garden for all seasons: rare plants and shrubs, especially primulas and rhododendrons, best seen *in early summer*. Tea room (see Pubs and Restaurants) children's trail, plant sales and boat trips. Excellent disabled access and mobility scooters available to borrow. *Open daily Mar-Nov 10.00-17.00 & Dec-Feb 10.00-16.00; also May-Aug, Wed-Thu until 21.00*. Charge.

● **Upton**
Norfolk. Stores. Scattered houses around a green with the church of St Margaret, a large Perpendicular building, standing apart to the south. Some of the pew ends are carved with poppy heads. A stone in the graveyard is carved with a wherry, the traditional Broadland sailing vessel. The community-run shop (www.whitehorseupton.com/uptonshop) is incorporated in the community pub and is *open daily 08.00-18.00 (Sat-Sun 16.00)*.

Palmers Hollow Post Mill Upton Dyke. A tiny hollow-post drainage windpump, unique in that it has a plunger action. In danger of being lost forever, it was moved here from Acle Marshes and restored by millwright Richard Seago. Private – but it can be viewed from the footpath in the village.

Clippesby Mill Just below the entrance to Upton Dyke. One of the older drainage windmills in the area, increased in height to 41ft in the mid 19thC. The mill has a four-story tapered brick tower with a weather-boarded, boat shaped cap and petticoat. Originally featuring a scoopwheel, it is now in residential use.

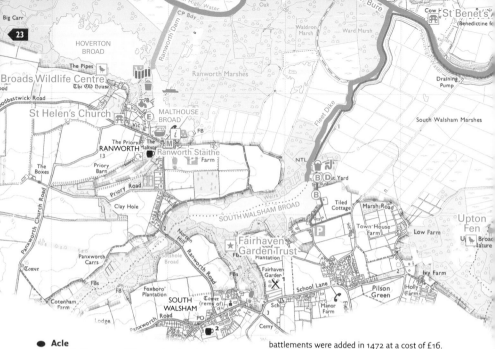

Acle

Norfolk. PO, stores, off-licence, chemist, takeaways, fish & chips, butcher, library, garage, station. Half way between Norwich and Great Yarmouth, Acle is a pleasant market town with some nice houses dotted around its centre. St Edmund's church has a round tower dating from 13th C – the battlements were added in 1472 at a cost of £16. The tall screen is very fine and the font, its stem adorned by four lions and four wild men, is dated 1410. Acle Bridge, a mile north east, was the site of many executions, the luckless criminals being hanged from the parapets. Concrete has replaced medieval stone but the ghosts apparently remain.

Pubs and Restaurants

✗ **1 Fairhaven Woodland and Water Garden Tea Room** School Road, South Walsham NR13 6DZ (01603 270449; www.fairhavengarden. co.uk). Family-friendly café, incorporated into a beautiful woodland and water garden, serving homemade pastries, hot food, light lunches and teas. Mooring. *Open daily 10.00-17.00.*

🍺✗ **2 The Ship Inn** 18 The Street, South Walsham NR13 6DQ (01603 270049; www. shipsouthwalsham.co.uk). First licenced in 1789, this pub serves real ale and food *Mon-Sat L and E & all day Sun.* Outside terrace and patio, dog-friendly. Wi-Fi. *Open daily 09.30-23.00 (Sun 22.30).*

🍺 **3 The White Horse** 17 Chapel Road, Upton NR13 6BT (01493 750696; www.whitehorseupton. com). 100% community-owned, this historic Broadlands pub, dating from 1798, is a short stroll from the idyllic Upton Marshes and a five-minute walk from Upton Staithe moorings. Real ales, real cider and appetising home-cooked food served *daily 12.00-21.00.* Garden, dog- and child-friendly. *Regular* live music. Traditional pub games, real fires and Wi-Fi. Camping. *Open 12.00-00.00.*

🍺✗ **4 The Lion Inn** Thurne The Street, Thurne NR29 3AP (01692 671806; www.thelionatthurne. com). Recently refurbished hostelry in a remote village, standing at the head of a short inlet, serving a selection of 24 beers and ciders. Food available *L and E.* Large garden, dog- and child-friendly. Traditional pub games and real fires. Camping nearby. *Open daily 12.00-23.00.* Telephone for *winter opening hours.*

✗🍷 **5 Pedro's** Acle New Road, Acle Bridge NR13 3AS (01493 750972; www.pedrosrestaurants. co.uk/acle). Wine, coffee and cocktails in a relaxed, welcoming tapas bar where the emphasis is on sharing. Families welcome. *Open L and E.*

🍺✗ **6 The Acle Bridge Inn** Acle Bridge, Old Road, Acle NR13 3AT (01493 750288; www. norfolkbroadsinns.co.uk). Riverside restaurant and bar, majoring on food – *daily 12.00-21.00* – also real ale. Children, dogs and muddy boots welcome. Large riverside garden. Mooring. Wi-Fi. *Open 11.00-23.00 (Sun 22.30).*

🍺✗ **7 The Kings Head** The Street, Acle NR13 3DY (01493 717892; www.facebook.com/ kingsheadacle). Welcoming, family-friendly pub in the heart of the village, serving real ales and food *L and E.* Garden. Sports TV. B&B. *Open daily 12.00-23.00 (Sun 22.30).*

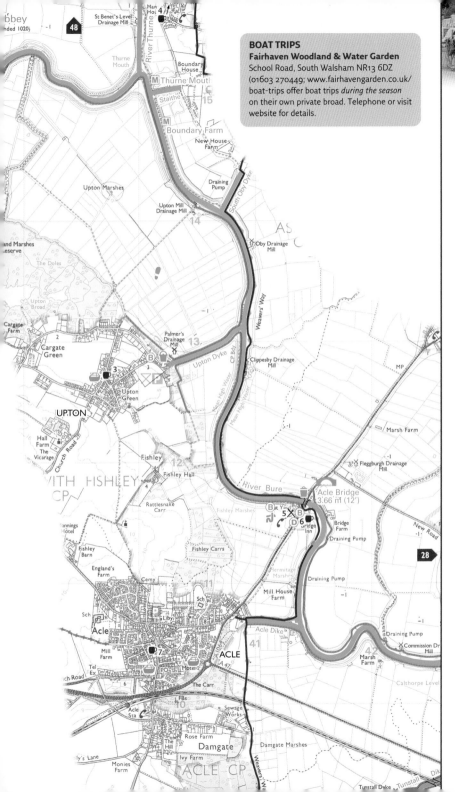

BOAT TRIPS
Fairhaven Woodland & Water Garden
School Road, South Walsham NR13 6DZ
(01603 270449; www.fairhavengarden.co.uk/
boat-trips offer boat trips *during the season*
on their own private broad. Telephone or visit
website for details.

Stracey Arms

The river passes the isolated village of Stokesby and soon resumes its lonely course until the main Norwich–Yarmouth road closes in at Stracey Arms. This is, however, but a brief encounter and once again the marshes dominate with the flat skyline broken only by the towers of ruined wind pumps and the distant chimneys of Great Yarmouth. Imperceptibly the river changes – the exposed riverbed becomes muddier and the piling heavier. The harbour of Great Yarmouth cannot be far away.

- **Stokesby**

Norfolk. Shop, PO box. A charming and virtually unspoilt red-brick riverside village. The thatched church of St Andrew is a short walk to the east. It is mainly Decorated and contains benches with openwork tracery backs, ends carved with poppy heads and arm rests with animals and a kneeling woman. There are some excellent brasses. Glebe farmhouse, across the road, has a medieval stone doorway. The shop is in the Ferry Inn, *open daily 08.00-18.00.*

Stracey Arms Windpump Mill House, New Road, Norwich NR13 3QE (07473 315441; www.facebook.com/straceyarms). Built on piles sunk some 40ft between the road and the river, this Grade II* pump was fully restored in 2019 with a £554,600 Heritage Lottery Fund grant. It was last used in 1940 as a fortified pillbox with gun loops cut into the tower to defend the local area. Built in 1883, it is a four-story drainage mill with a tapering red-brick tower and boat-shaped weather boarded cap. Shop and tearoom. *Open daily.*

- **Runham**

Norfolk. Farm shop. A small farming community. Set apart to the east is the church of St Peter and St Paul, its north tower topped with battlements and pinnacles. Parts of the building date from 14thC. The farm shop is *open daily 08.00-17.00* – Poplar Farm,

Church Lane NR29 3EL (07827 541695; www.facebook.com/PoplarFarmProduce).

Ormesby, Rollesby and Filby Broads Lying about 3½ miles south east of Heigham Bridge or 3 miles east of Acle Bridge. Known as the 'Trinity Broads' these isolated but very beautiful broads were designated an SSSI in 1998 and they abound with wildlife. Their surrounding villages are a fascinating area well-worth exploring. For buses in the area see www.sanderscoaches.com/timetables/6-X6-6a.

- **Rollesby**

Norfolk. Farm shop. A quiet village west of Ormesby Broad with rowing boat hire *in the summer.* The church of St George has a round Norman tower, the rest of the building being of 14thC origin. The farm shop is *open daily 09.00-18.00* and offers pick-your-own during the fruit growing season – The Tacons The Grange, Rollesby NR29 5AJ (01493 740236; www.thetacons.co.uk).

- **Ormesby St Margaret (and St Michael)**

Norfolk. PO, Stores, off-licence, takeaways, fish & chips, garage. A larger village to the east of the Broad with some handsome houses. The church has a perpendicular battlemented tower and a Norman south doorway. Ormesby St Michael lies closest to Rollesby Broad.

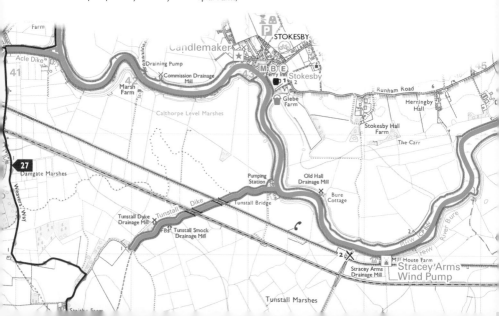

● **Filby**
Norfolk. PO, stores, off-licence. A pretty village with some charming old cottages. The church is worth a second look – inside this Decorated building you will find a fine rood screen with eight painted saints and no less than seven locks on the belfry door, which was probably once used as a strong room. The north door is embellished with foliate 14th-C ironwork.

Thrigby Hall Wildlife Gardens Filby Road, Thrigby, Great Yarmouth NR29 3DR (01493 369477; www.thrigbyhall.com). Beautifully landscaped gardens and a specialised collection of animals, birds and reptiles. Attractions include a Willow Pattern Garden, Lime Tree Lookout and Tiger Tree Walkway constructed in the tree tops above the tigers' enclosure. Wheelchair access. *Open all year, daily from 10.00.* Parking and children's play areas free. Charge for admission to Wildlife Garden.

Caistor Castle and Motor Museum Castle Lane, Caistor-on-Sea, Great Yarmouth NR30 5SN (www.caistercastle.co.uk). An impressive 15thC moated castle built for Sir John Fastolf, who successfully led the English archers at Agincourt and accumulated great wealth as a result of fighting the French. It passed in his will to the Pastons on his death in 1459 (John Paston was his lawyer and Fastolf's heirs disputed the legacy for many years) and they lived there, with a short break, until 1599. Views from the 100ft tower are excellent. The Castle is currently home to the largest private collection of motor vehicles in Britain, which is housed in a purpose-built museum and includes many fine and rare veteran, vintage, classic, sports and touring automobiles and motorcycles. It includes an 1893 Panhard et Levassor, the first real car in the world. *Open Sun-Fri 10.00-16.30.* Charge.

Caister Roman Fort Norwich Road, Caister-on-Sea NR30 5RN (0370 333 1181). Remains of a Roman 'Saxon Shore' fort, including foundations and sections of wall and ditch. The fort was constructed around AD 200, for a unit of the Roman army and navy, and occupied until the end of the 4th C. Well-behaved dogs welcome. *Access at all reasonable times.* Free.

BOAT TRIPS
The Waterside Inn, Main Road, Rollesby NR29 5EF (01493 740531; www.thewatersiderollesby. co.uk/Boating) offers 30-minute boat trips during the season in its Edwardian launch *Gentleman Jim*: 1st trip *11.00 and last trip 16.25* (weather-dependent). Also rowing- and electrically-propelled dinghies for hire *by the hour or the half day from 11.00-16.00.* No dogs.

WALKING AND CYCLING
The Broads by Bike (www.thebroadsbybike. org.uk/page) is a comprehensive list of circular cycle routes and cycle hire centres. NCN30 runs through Ormesby.

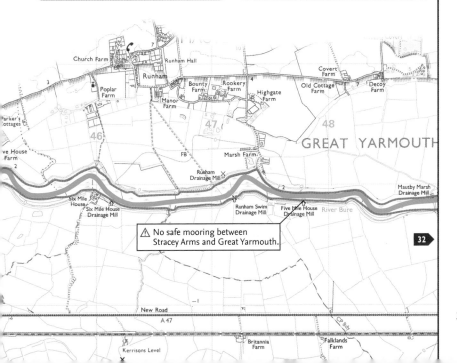

⚠ No safe mooring between Stracey Arms and Great Yarmouth.

1 The Ferry Inn River Front, The Green, Stokesby NR29 3EX (01493 751096; www.facebook.com/theferryinnstokesby). Isolated but in an idyllic setting, this gem of a pub serves real ales and traditional fare *daily 08.00-21.00. Breakfast served 08.00-11.00.* Riverside garden, dog- and family-friendly. Traditional pub games, real fires and Wi-Fi. Mooring. *Open 08.00-23.00.*

2 Stracey Arms Mill Shop & Tea Rooms Mill House, New Road, Tunstall NR13 3QE (07473 315441; www.facebook.com/straceyarms). Built in 1883 and served as a pillbox during WWII, the mill is now home to a well-stocked shop and welcoming tea rooms rather than a battery of anti-aircraft guns! Telephone for *opening times.*

3 The Waterside Rollesby Main Road, Rollesby NR29 5EF (01493 740531; www.thewatersiderollesby.co.uk). Serving an extensive selection of homemade cakes, teas and light lunches by day, this Broadside restaurant becomes, on occasions, a haven for fine dining at night. *Open Apr-Sep 09.00-17.00 & Oct-Mar 10.00-15.00.* Also boat trips on Edwardian launch *Gentleman Jim* and dinghies for hire.

4 The Boathouse Eels Foot Road, Ormesby St Michael NR29 3LP (01493 730342; www.theboathouseormesbybroad.co.uk). Situated in 11 acres of grounds, on the banks of Ormesby Broad, this establishment serves superb, freshly-prepared food *L and E* together with a small but ever-changing range of real ales. B&B

5 Filby Bridge Restaurant Main Road, Filby Bridge NR29 3AA (01493 368142; www.facebook.com/filbybridge). First class food and superb views over Trinity Broads served in a family-owned restaurant. Extensive menu including a selection of seafood & fish dishes, various steak specialities, seasonal produce and homemade desserts. *Open Tue-Sun L and E (not Sun E).*

6 The Smokehouse Yarmouth Road, Ormesby St Margaret NR29 3QG (01493 731877; www.facebook.com/smokehouseormesby). Welcoming, family-friendly establishment, Serving a large range of barbequed and smoked delights, together with burgers, hot dogs, steaks, ribs and chicken. *Open daily 12.00-22.00.*

7 The Kings Arms Main Road, Fleggburgh NR29 3AG (01493 368333; www.kingsarmsfleggburgh.com). Large two-bar hostelry dispensing real ale and traditional pub food *L and E (not Sun E).* Garden, dog- and child-friendly. *Regular* live music. Real fires and Wi-Fi. Camping nearby. *Open 12.00-22.00 (Fri-Sat 00.00).*

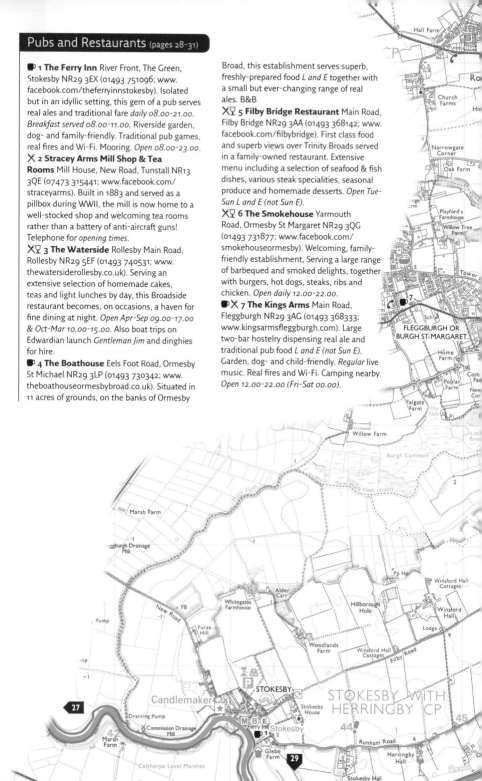

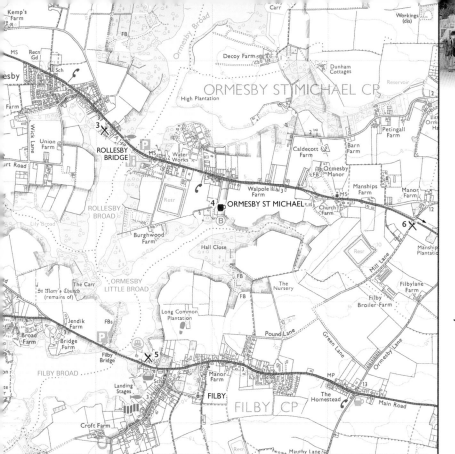

DWILE FLONKING

Also known as dwyle flunking, this arcane pub sport is also played as far afield as the Lewes Arms, in Sussex, although its more fanatical proponents claim antecedents extending way back to 16th C, as depicted in a Brueghel the Elder painting of that time. Either way, it is clearly well established in parts of East Anglia, whose chief protagonists maintain that the rules of the game are impenetrable and that the result is always hotly contested. However, according to the Friends of the Lewes Arms, approximate rules (now enshrined in Wikipedia) are as follows:

A dull-witted person is chosen as the 'jobanowl' (referee) and the two teams decide who flonks first by tossing a sugar beet. The game begins when the jobanowl shouts "Here y'go t'gither!"

The non-flonking team joins hands and dances in a circle around a member of the flonking team, a practice known as 'girting'. The flonker dips his dwile-tipped 'driveller' (a 1–2 ft long hazel stick) into a bucket of beer, then spins around in the opposite direction to the girters and flonks (flings) his dwile (floor cloth) at them.

If the dwile misses completely it is known as a 'swadge'. When this happens, the flonker must drink the contents of an ale-filled 'gazunder' (chamber pot) before the wet dwile has passed from hand to hand along the line of now non-girting girters, chanting the ceremonial mantra of 'pot' 'pot' 'pot'.

A full game comprises two 'snurds', each snurd being one team taking a turn at girting. The jobanowl adds interest and difficulty to the game by randomly switching the direction of rotation and will levy drinking penalties on any player found not taking the game seriously enough.

Points are awarded as follows:

+3 for a wanton: a direct hit on a girter's head

+2 for a morther: a body hit

+1 for a ripper: a leg hit

Minus 1 per sober person at the end of the game when the team with the most points wins, and will be awarded a ceremonial pewter gazunder.

An excellent British Pathé newsreel clip, dating back to 1967 and depicting this ancient pastime, can be found at: www.youtube.com/watch?v=UBamCWdx6gl.

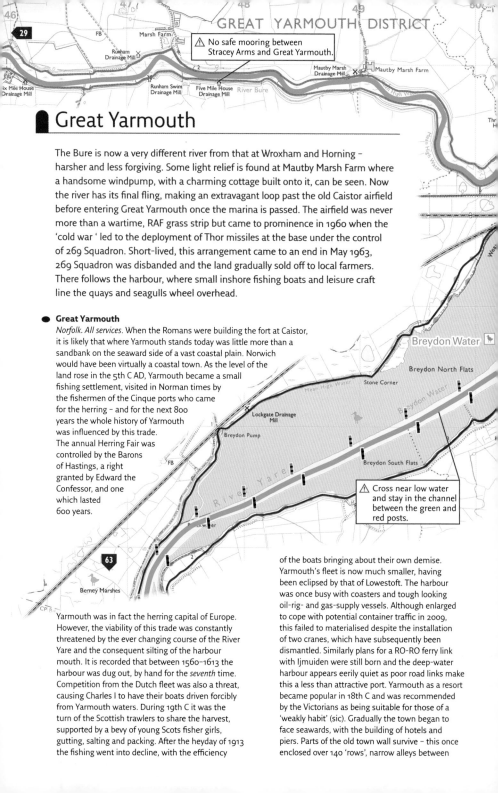

29

FB · Marsh Farm

Runham Drainage Mill

⚠ No safe mooring between
Stracey Arms and Great Yarmouth.

Mautby Marsh Drainage Mill ✕ Mautby Marsh Farm

ix Mile House Drainage Mill

Runham Swim Drainage Mill · Five Mile House Drainage Mill · River Bure

Great Yarmouth

The Bure is now a very different river from that at Wroxham and Horning –
harsher and less forgiving. Some light relief is found at Mautby Marsh Farm where
a handsome windpump, with a charming cottage built onto it, can be seen. Now
the river has its final fling, making an extravagant loop past the old Caistor airfield
before entering Great Yarmouth once the marina is passed. The airfield was never
more than a wartime, RAF grass strip but came to prominence in 1960 when the
'cold war ' led to the deployment of Thor missiles at the base under the control
of 269 Squadron. Short-lived, this arrangement came to an end in May 1963,
269 Squadron was disbanded and the land gradually sold off to local farmers.
There follows the harbour, where small inshore fishing boats and leisure craft
line the quays and seagulls wheel overhead.

● Great Yarmouth

Norfolk. All services. When the Romans were building the fort at Caistor,
it is likely that where Yarmouth stands today was little more than a
sandbank on the seaward side of a vast coastal plain. Norwich
would have been virtually a coastal town. As the level of the
land rose in the 5th C AD, Yarmouth became a small
fishing settlement, visited in Norman times by
the fishermen of the Cinque ports who came
for the herring – and for the next 800
years the whole history of Yarmouth
was influenced by this trade.
The annual Herring Fair was
controlled by the Barons
of Hastings, a right
granted by Edward the
Confessor, and one
which lasted
600 years.

Breydon Water

Breydon North Flats

Stone Corner

Breydon Water

Mean High Water

Lockgate Drainage Mill

Breydon Pump

FB

Breydon South Flats

River Yare

⚠ Cross near low water
and stay in the channel
between the green and
red posts.

63

Berney Marshes

CP R

Yarmouth was in fact the herring capital of Europe.
However, the viability of this trade was constantly
threatened by the ever changing course of the River
Yare and the consequent silting of the harbour
mouth. It is recorded that between 1560–1613 the
harbour was dug out, by hand for the *seventh* time.
Competition from the Dutch fleet was also a threat,
causing Charles I to have their boats driven forcibly
from Yarmouth waters. During 19th C it was the
turn of the Scottish trawlers to share the harvest,
supported by a bevy of young Scots fisher girls,
gutting, salting and packing. After the heyday of 1913
the fishing went into decline, with the efficiency

of the boats bringing about their own demise.
Yarmouth's fleet is now much smaller, having
been eclipsed by that of Lowestoft. The harbour
was once busy with coasters and tough looking
oil-rig- and gas-supply vessels. Although enlarged
to cope with potential container traffic in 2009,
this failed to materialised despite the installation
of two cranes, which have subsequently been
dismantled. Similarly plans for a RO-RO ferry link
with Ijmuiden were still born and the deep-water
harbour appears eerily quiet as poor road links make
this a less than attractive port. Yarmouth as a resort
became popular in 18th C and was recommended
by the Victorians as being suitable for those of a
'weakly habit' (sic). Gradually the town began to
face seawards, with the building of hotels and
piers. Parts of the old town wall survive – this once
enclosed over 140 'rows', narrow alleys between

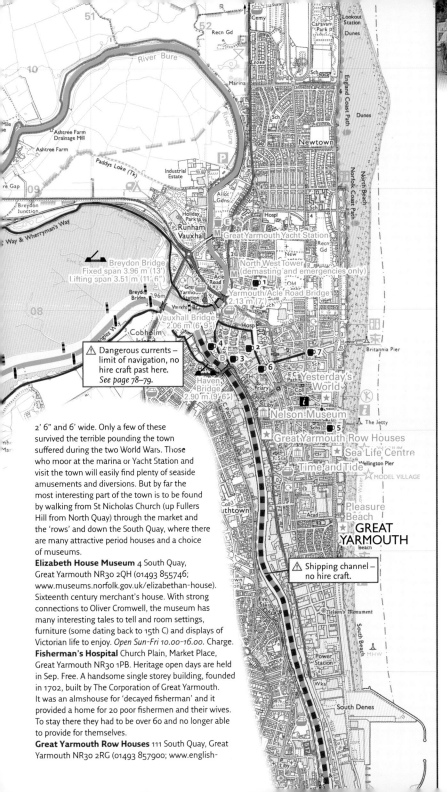

2' 6" and 6' wide. Only a few of these survived the terrible pounding the town suffered during the two World Wars. Those who moor at the marina or Yacht Station and visit the town will easily find plenty of seaside amusements and diversions. But by far the most interesting part of the town is to be found by walking from St Nicholas Church (up Fullers Hill from North Quay) through the market and the 'rows' and down the South Quay, where there are many attractive period houses and a choice of museums.

Elizabeth House Museum 4 South Quay, Great Yarmouth NR30 2QH (01493 855746; www.museums.norfolk.gov.uk/elizabethan-house). Sixteenth century merchant's house. With strong connections to Oliver Cromwell, the museum has many interesting tales to tell and room settings, furniture (some dating back to 15th C) and displays of Victorian life to enjoy. *Open Sun-Fri 10.00-16.00.* Charge.

Fisherman's Hospital Church Plain, Market Place, Great Yarmouth NR30 1PB. Heritage open days are held in Sep. Free. A handsome single storey building, founded in 1702, built by The Corporation of Great Yarmouth. It was an almshouse for 'decayed fisherman' and it provided a home for 20 poor fishermen and their wives. To stay there they had to be over 60 and no longer able to provide for themselves.

Great Yarmouth Row Houses 111 South Quay, Great Yarmouth NR30 2RG (01493 857900; www.english-

Sailing at Horning

heritage.org.uk/visit/places/great-yarmouth-row-houses-and-greyfriars-cloisters). The narrow lanes of the Yarmouth Rows, a feature of the older part of the town, were originally a network of alleyways connecting the dwellings crammed inside Yarmouth's town walls. Many of the Row houses were damaged by World War II bombing or demolished after the war, but these surviving dwellings have been restored as fascinating museums. *Opening times vary according to the season, so telephone or visit the website for details*. Charge.

Greyfriars' Cloisters Close to the Rows stands Greyfriars' Cloisters, the remains of a 13th-century friary of Franciscan 'grey friars', later converted into a number of Row dwellings. You can still see traces of their interior features, revealed by the wartime bombing, on the walls of the cloister and church.

Hippodrome Circus St George's Road, Great Yarmouth NR30 2EU (01493 844172; www.hippodromecircus.co.uk). An Art Nouveau delight, built by the showman George Gilbert in 1903 and designed by architect Ralph Scott Cockrill. It is one of only two purpose-built permanent circuses in England still in operation, and one of only three in the world with a circus floor that sinks into a pool, last operated c2007. The Hippodrome is home to the backstage museum of memorabilia, displaying over 100 years of circus activity which also offers the opportunity to see the original water mechanism and tanks and peruse the engine room diaries kept 1930-70.

Joyland Amusement Park Marine Parade, Great Yarmouth NR30 2EH (01493 644094; www.joyland.org.uk). Opened in 1949 on the site of the former Anchor Gardens next to Britannia Pier, Joyland has always been owned and operated by the Cole family. Engineering entrepreneur Horace Cole designed the world famous Snails and the now unique Tyrolean Tubs and these were built at the family engineering works at Steam Mill Lane in Great Yarmouth called H Cole and Co. It is fantastic testament to Horace that both the Snails and Tubs remain in operation today and are still as popular today with young and old alike. A ore recent addition is the American Diner. *Opening times vary according to the season, so telephone or visit the website for details*. Charge.

Jurassic Journey Tower complex, Marine Parade, Great Yarmouth NR30 2EW (01493 852239; www.jurassic-journey.co.uk). Jurassic Journey is an adventure back in time to when dinosaurs ruled the earth. Aimed at family audiences – with over 10 impressive installations of animated dinosaurs with electronic moving parts and lots of other interesting and interactive displays – the dinosaurs really do come to life. A chance to experience up-close encounters with a lifelike Stegosaurus, Velociraptor and the king T-Rex. *Open daily 10.00-16.00*. Charge.

Merrivale Model Village Marine Parade, Great Yarmouth NR30 3JG (01493 842097; www.merrivalemodelvillage.co.uk). Pretty much 'what it says on the tin' including the famous garden, railway, crazy golf, tea rooms and gift shop. Also the Williamson's Old Penny 'end-of-the-pier' Arcade where you can enjoy playing machines such as One Arm Bandits, 'operate' Working Models, try Allwins Strength Testers and indulge the Fortune Tellers – to name but a few! *Open daily 10.00-17.00*. Charge.

Old Merchant's House, The Row 111, Houses and Greyfriars Off South Quay. A worthwhile tour starting at the Row 111 houses. The Old Merchant's House is a Grade II* 17th-C brick building with wooden mullioned windows. Inside is a collection of 17th – 18th-C domestic ironwork. To take the tour visit www.nationaltrust.org.uk/elizabethan-house-museum/trails/great-yarmouth-heritage-trail.

Pleasure Beach South Beach Parade, Great Yarmouth NR30 3EH (01493 844585; www.pleasure-beach.co.uk). Historic seaside pleasure park, first opened in 1909, and operating ever since. The most popular ride is the roller coaster, opening in 1932 and still going strong. There are now plenty more white-knuckle rides to keep it company. Charge.

Sea Life Aquarium Marine Parade, Great Yarmouth NR30 3AH (01493 330631; www.visitsealife.com/great-yarmouth). Many native species and a tropical ocean display. Visitors can get up close and eyeball all kinds of underwater creatures, from shrimps to sharks. And everything else from jelly invaders to penguins. *Opening times vary according to the season, so telephone or visit the website for details*. Charge.

South Quay NR30 2QH. Some fine period houses, including the Customs House, built by John Andrews, 'the greatest herring merchant in Europe' in 1720.

St Nicholas Church South Plain, Great Yarmouth NR30 1NE (01493 858410; https://www.exploringnorfolkchurches.org/church/great-yarmouth-minster-st-nicholas-great-yarmouth). Based on plan area, the third largest parish church in England, dating from 12th C and once attached to

NAVIGATIONAL NOTES

1 Tides: If you are uncertain about tide times for your passage onto Breydon Water, tie up at Great Yarmouth Yacht Station and check. Ideally you should pass through the harbour *within one hour after low water slack*, thus avoiding problems with strong currents and low bridges. See diagrams on page(s) 78-79.

2 Breydon Water: Under all circumstances stay in the marked channel between the posts.

3 Pleasure craft are not encouraged to use the harbour, due to the fierce currents in the river and should berth at the Yacht Station on the River Bure.

4 Hire craft are not permitted below Haven Bridge.

5 The Breydon Bridge keeper can be contacted on VHF channel 12 if a lift is required for a tall mast etc.

a Benedictine Priory. Having been restored from a ruined condition in 1847 and 1862, it was gutted by fire in 1942. During the period 1957–60 it was rebuilt within the 13th-C walls in a disappointing imitation Gothic. The result is impressive but lacking in authenticity and coherent style. Café and children's area. *Open Mon-Fri 09.00-15.00 & Sat 10.00-13.00.*

The Piers. Wellington Pier was built in 1853 and the Grade II Britannia Pier in 1857 (rebuilt in 1901). The latter still hosts one of the few end-of-pier theatres left in the country while its companion building, at the end of Wellington Pier, was demolished in 2005 to be replaced by a family entertainment centre three years later. The Jetty dates from 1560, having since been rebuilt and extended several times.

Time and Tide Museum of Great Yarmouth Life Blackfriars' Road, Great Yarmouth NR30 3BX (01493 743930; www.museums.norfolk.gov.uk/time-tide). Norfolk's third largest museum, set in a very well preserved Victorian herring curing works, and the opportunity to follow Great Yarmouth's transformation from sandbank to the present day. Discover the town's fascinating history and contemporary life, its rich maritime and fishing heritage, some of the colourful characters who made their living from the sea and the people who live in Yarmouth now. Wander through a Victorian 'Row' and see inside a fisherman's home. Experience the heady atmosphere of a 1950s quayside, take the wheel of a coastal drifter and hear gripping tales of wreck and rescue on the high seas. *Open daily. Charge.*

Tolhouse Museum 12 Tolhouse St, Great Yarmouth NR30 2SQ (01493 858900; www.museums.norfolk. uk/tolhouse-gaol). Enjoy displays, hands-on activities and the chance to find out about the history of this 12th-C medieval merchant's house, which was transformed into one of the town's most important civic buildings. Visit one of the oldest prisons in the country and explore Great Yarmouth's story of crime and punishment. Discover the fate of thieves, smugglers, witches, pirates and murderers when punishment included transportation and execution. *Open daily.* Charge.

Venetian Waterways and Gardens North Drive, Great Yarmouth NR30 (www.venetianwaterways.com). The Waterways is a seven-acre park comprising of the Venetian Waterways, the Ornamental Gardens and Boating Lake, located just north of Great Yarmouth's Golden Mile. The Venetian Waterways 'canals' serpentine their way through the park crossed and re-crossed by bridges, creating interlinked islands throughout, alongside which numerous ornamental features and structures can be found. The Boating Lake, a man-made attraction, is the last of its kind in the region. A popular haven for ducks and herons, the park is a tranquil place for visitors to stop and relax for a while, to take a ride on the water or to enjoy exploring the plant life. Café. *Open 24 hours. Free.*

Winter Gardens South Beach Parade, Great Yarmouth NR30 3JF. A striking Grade II listed building, constructed in glass and iron. Fabricated in Torquay and moved to Great Yarmouth in 1904 it had, by 2018, been listed by the Victorian Society amongst the top ten most endangered buildings in Great Britain. By the time you are reading this it may, sadly, be no more. However, an ambitious project is underway to restore and reimagine the Winter Gardens, placing it at the heart of the town's regeneration and making it a central feature of its daily life.

Tourist Information Centre Maritime House, 25 Marine Parade, Great Yarmouth, Norfolk, NR30 2EN. *Open daily 10.00-16.30 (Sun 16.00).*

Pubs and Restaurants (pages 32–33)

⬤✕ **1 The King's Arms** 229 Northgate Street, Great Yarmouth NR30 1BG (01493 843736; www. thekingsarmsgreatyarmouth.co.uk). Featuring an elaborately carved Royal Arms from a previous 19th-C building, this friendly, welcoming hostelry serves real ale and food *Sun-Fri L and E (not Sun E)* and *Sat 12.00-20.00.* Garden, dog- and child-friendly. Traditional pub games, newspapers, real fires and sports TV. *Open Sun-Tue & Wed-Sat 12.00-23.00 (Fri-Sat 00.00).*

⬤✕ **2 The Feathers Hotel** 1 Market Gates, Great Yarmouth NR30 2BG (01493 844024). Close to the market place, this pub serves competitively-priced real ale. Outside seating, family-friendly. *Regular* live music and sports TV. *Open Mon-Sat 11.00-23.00 & Sun 12.00-22.30.*

⬤✕ **3 The Star Hotel** 24 Hall Quay, Great Yarmouth NR30 1HG (01493 842294). Built as a merchant's house in 1694 – becoming a hotel in 1865 – this comfortable hostelry, with its wood-panelled rooms, serves real ale and food *L and E. Open daily 12.00-23.00.*

⬤ **4 Tombstone Brewery & Saloon Bar** 6 George Street, Great Yarmouth NR30 1HR (07584 504444; www.tombstonebrewery.co.uk). Award-winning pub, home to the local Tombstone Brewery, dispensing a wide range of real ales (up to six of their own) and real ciders. Dog-friendly and traditional pub games.

Open Mon-Sat 12.00-21.00 (Thu-Sat 23.00) & Sun 12.00-18.00.

⬤✕ **5 The Barking Smack** 16 Marine Parade, Great Yarmouth NR30 3AH (01493 859752/07754 116172; www.barkingsmack.com). Sea-front pub with an elaborately carved bar, majoring on Continental and international beers, many of them on draught. Also, real ales and ciders from closer to home. Patio and *summer* barbeques. Food available *daily 12.00-18.00.* Dog- and family-friendly. Wi-Fi. *Open 12.00-23.00 (Fri-Sat 00.00). Closed Nov-Mar.*

⬤ **6 The Mariners** 69 Howard Street South, Great Yarmouth NR30 1LN (01493 331164; www. facebook.com/marinerstavern). Family-run local, serving a wide range of real ales (many from local microbreweries) and cider, this traditional town-centre hostelry has a family room, real fires and pub games. Outside seating, dog- and child-friendly. Wi-Fi. *Open daily 12.00-00.00.*

⬤ **7 The Troll Cart** 7 Regent Road, Great Yarmouth NR30 2AF (01493 332932). Named after the narrow, horse drawn vehicles that were used to navigate the Rows of the town and, for once, not a conversion of an old, redundant building, this 1996-built establishment dispensing inexpensive real ales, real cider and food *daily 08.00-23.00.* Patio seating, family-friendly. Wi-Fi. B&B. *Open 08.00-00.00.*

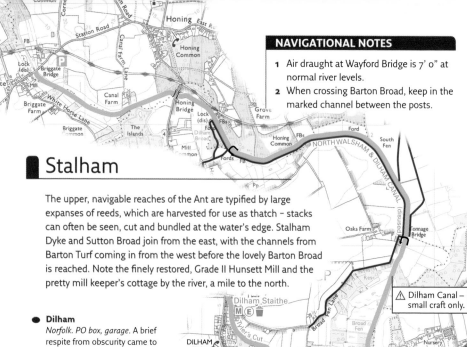

NAVIGATIONAL NOTES

1 Air draught at Wayford Bridge is 7' 0" at normal river levels.
2 When crossing Barton Broad, keep in the marked channel between the posts.

Stalham

The upper, navigable reaches of the Ant are typified by large expanses of reeds, which are harvested for use as thatch – stacks can often be seen, cut and bundled at the water's edge. Stalham Dyke and Sutton Broad join from the east, with the channels from Barton Turf coming in from the west before the lovely Barton Broad is reached. Note the finely restored, Grade II Hunsett Mill and the pretty mill keeper's cottage by the river, a mile to the north.

⚠ Dilham Canal – small craft only.

● **Dilham**

Norfolk. PO box, garage. A brief respite from obscurity came to Dilham with the opening of the North Walsham & Dilham Canal on 29th August 1826. Regrettably the venture was never a financial success and the last wherry took a cargo from Bacton Wood Staithe in 1934. Since then the canal and the village have remained very much a backwater.

● **Stalham**

Norfolk. PO, stores, off-licence, chemist, takeaways, fish & chips, library, garage. Stalham Staithe is a popular holiday venue, separated from this busy Georgian Market town by the main A149 road. The squat, mainly Decorated church of St Mary contains a remarkable 15th-C font, standing on three steps, one decorated with a Catherine wheel motif. The Trinity, Christ's baptism and the 12 Apostles are depicted on the bowl. Stores *open 08.00-22.00 (Sun 10.00-16.00).*

Museum of the Broads The Poor's, Staithe Road, Stalham, Norwich NR12 9DA (01692 581681; www. museumofthebroads.org.uk). An independent museum located at the historic and picturesque staithe offering a view of Broadlands life. Family-friendly trails and activities for children, together with trips on the steam boat *Falcon (Tue-Thu). Open Jul-Sep, Sun-Fri 10.00-16.30 & Sat 10.00-13.00 and Oct, Sun-Thu 10.00-16.00 & Sat 10.00-13.00.* Charge.

Stalham Old Firehouse Museum 118 High Street, Stalham NR12 9AZ (01692 582781; www. norfolkbroads.com/link/stalham-firehouse-museum-897). Photographs, artefacts and a 1902 horse-drawn fire engine housed in the country's second-oldest firehouse: a tiny Grade II listed building. *Open Easter-Sep, Tue & Thu-Fri 10.00-*

12.00 and 14.00-16.00. Telephone to confirm opening times. Free (donations welcome).

● **Sutton**

Norfolk. PO box. The village lies to the east of Sutton Staithe, across the main A149 road, at the head of Sutton Broad. To maintain a clear channel, a crop of reeds is regularly taken for thatch. The small church of St Michael, to the east of the main street, dates from 14thC.

● **Barton Turf**

Norfolk. PO box. A tiny village whose origins must lie in the seasonal migration to dig peat (or turf) but whose pride must rest in its church, St Michael. The large west tower has a superb entrance door, but of particular interest is the rood screen, considered by some to be amongst the finest in England. Dating from 15thC, the paintings depict three saints and a set of Heavenly Hierarchies (or order of angels). There is also a fine brass to Thomas Amys, 1445. Barton Broad is a 400-acre nature reserve administered by Norfolk Wildlife Trust. Once bypassed by the Ant, the river was diverted to flow through it.

Pubs and Restaurants

◆╳ **1 The Lighthouse Inn** Coast Road, Walcott NR12 0PE (01692 650371; www.lighthouseinn.co.uk). Busy, family-oriented pub, catering predominantly for the seasonal trade, serving real ale and food *daily 12.00-21.00*. Garden, dog- and child-friendly. Traditional pub games and real fires. Camping nearby. *Open 11.00-23.00*.

◆╳ **2 The Star Inn & Restaurant** School Road, Star Hill, Lessingham NR12 0DN (01692 580510; www.thestarlessingham.co.uk). Welcoming village local, serving real ales and cider, together with excellent home-cooked meals and bar snacks *Tue-Sun L and E (not Sun E)*. Large beer garden, dogs welcome. Traditional pub games, real fires and Wi-Fi. B&B. *Open Tue-Sun L and E*.

◆ **3 The Cross Keys** The Street, Dilham NR28 9PS (01692 536398; www.crosskeysdilham.co.uk). Traditional village local, a short walk from delightful moorings on the River Ant, dispensing real ale and food *L and E*. Garden, dog-friendly. Traditional pub games, real fires, sports TV and Wi-Fi. Camping. *Open 12.00-00.00. Closes at 22.00 out of season.*

◆╳ **4 The Smallburgh Crown** North Walsham Road, Smallburgh NR12 9AD (01692 536314; www.smallburghcrown.co.uk). This partially thatched, 15th-C coaching inn serves a good range of real ales, cider

and appetising food *daily 12.00-21.00*. Garden, dog-friendly. Traditional pub games, real fires and Wi-Fi. B&B. Camping nearby. *Open 11.45-23.00*.

◆╳ **5 The Wayford Bridge Hotel** Yarmouth Road, Wayford Bridge NR12 9LL (01692 582414; www.wayfordbridge.co.uk). Busy, family-oriented bar, restaurant and hotel serving real ale and food *Mon-Fri L and E; Sat-Sun 12.00-21.00*. B&B. *Open daily 12.00-23.00*.

◆ **6 The Grebe Hotel** 123 High Street, Stalham NR12 9BB (01692 583228). Comfortable town pub with two bars serving real ale. Wi-Fi. *Open 12.00-23.00 (Sun 22.30)*.

◆ **7 The Swan Inn** 90 High Street, Stalham NR12 9AU (01692 582829; www.facebook.com/stalhamswan). Locals two-bar pub serving real ale and food *L and E*. Traditional pub games and sports TV. *Open 12.00-23.00 (Sun 22.30)*.

◆╳ **8 The Harnser** Old Yarmouth Road, Stalham NR12 9QA (01692 580347; www.theharnser.co.uk). Single bar local with a pool table serving real ale

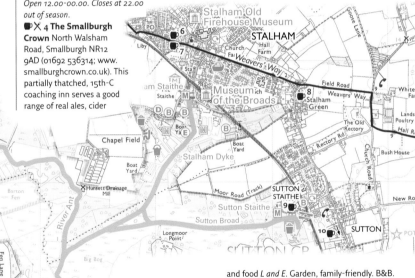

and food *L and E*. Garden, family-friendly. B&B. *Open 12.00-23.00 (Sun 22.30)*.

◆╳ **9 Sutton Staithe Hotel** Staithe Road, Sutton, Stalham NR12 9QS (01692 580244; www.suttonstaithehotel.co.uk). Cosy, beamed pub serving real ale and food *L and E*. Family-friendly. Real fires. B&B. *Open 12.00-23.00 (Sun 22.30)*.

◆╳ **10 The Crown Inn** The Street, Catfield NR29 5AA (01692 580128; www.catfieldcrown.co.uk). Comfortable, 300-year-old traditional village local, serving real ales and excellent home-cooked food with an Italian influence *L and E (not Mon E)*. Good selection of malt whiskies and bourbons. Garden, dog-friendly. Traditional pub games, real fires and Wi-Fi. Two cottages for rent. *Open Mon-Sat L and E & Sun 12.00-22.30*.

Irstead

The western end of Barton Broad extends to Neatishead: the narrow southern exit is marked by a large sign – it would otherwise be easily missed. Continuing south, the amiable mixture of carr woodland and open fields makes for a lively journey. At How Hill two fine wind pumps are passed before Ludham Bridge is approached. Once through, the views across miles of open farmland are splendid – the mill of At Benet's Abbey Gatehouse being clearly visible, indicating the proximity of the parent river.

● **Neatishead**
Norfolk. Stores, off-licence. A charming Georgian village to the west of Barton Broad. Community stores *open Mon-Sat 08.30-13.00 & 13.30-17.00 and Sun 08.30-12.00.*

RAF Air Defence Radar Museum Birds Lane, Near Horning NR12 8YB (01692 631485; www. radarmuseum.co.uk). An award-winning museum illustrating the history and development of air defence radar since its invention in 1935, located on an ex-RAF base. Visitors can explore the history and development of detection, air intelligence photography, radar an air battle management, from the 1930s through to today's computer technology. Lots of hands-on exhibits and a recreated operation's room. Free, guided tours, souvenir shop, café and picnic areas. *Open Apr-Oct, Tue-Sat 10.00-17.00 & B Hol Mon.* Charge (children under 7 free).

● **Irstead**
Norfolk. PO box. A tiny settlement with a fine river frontage around the thatched church of St Michael. Mainly Decorated, it has a fine 14th-C octagonal font depicting the Head of Christ, the Hand of God and leaf motifs on a stem with eight statuettes. The bench ends are carved with poppy heads and the rood screen has three saints painted on a light background. Note the medieval ironwork on the south door.

How Hill Nature Reserve (How Hill Trust). A microcosm of Broadland habitat – reed and sedge beds, marshland fields, clear dykes, carr woodland. The estate also includes Reedham Water and Cromes Broad. A tiny thatched cottage – Toad Hall – was once the home of the local marshman and is now a museum dedicated to 19th-C life on the Broads. Also the Turf Fen Drainage Museum: a striking windmill and the place to discover more about the evolution of the Broads and how today's landscape was created. The nature trails are *open all year.* Woodlands, gardens, tearooms and Norfolk Broads Study Centre.

Boardman's Mill On the How Hill estate, This mill was originally fitted with a scoopwheel but this was later replaced with a turbine pump. The mill ceased working in 1938 when it was blown over in a gale. Subsequently restored by Norfolk Windmills Trust and designated Grade II*, the pump is now complete with cap and non-working sails.

Turf Fen Wind Pump Also on the How Hill estate. This two-floor, boat-capped, double scoop wind pump was completed around 1875 and although of only two floors, it stood 31' high. Unusual in that each scoop can work independently of one another. Grade II listed, the mill is intact but without sails and currently appears somewhat run down.

● **Ludham Bridge**
Norfolk. Stores, off-licence, takeaway. Useful for supplies. Stores *open daily 07.30-17.00.*

Pubs and Restaurants (pages xx-xx)

🍺✕ **1 The White Horse** Inn The Street, Neatishead NR12 8AD (01692 630828; www. thewhitehorseinnneatishead.com). Delightful village pub and restaurant majoring on real ale, craft and bottled beers. Wide range of bar and restaurant food served *L and E*: freshly prepared and sourced from local suppliers. Courtyard seating, child- and dog-friendly. Traditional pub games, real fires and Wi-Fi. Camping nearby. *Open 11.00-23.00 (Sun 22.30).*

✕ **2 Wayfarer's Café** Ludham Bridge NR29 5NX (01692 630238; www.facebook.com/wayfarerscafe). Situated beside the picturesque River Ant, serving a wide range of hot and cold meals *L and E*, an *all day* breakfast and a takeaway service. Mooring.

🍺 **3 The Dog Inn** Johnsons Street, Ludham NR29 5NY (01692 630321; www.thedogpub. co.uk). Beautifully renovated pub, dispensing real ales and a wide range of locally-sourced, freshly prepared-food available *12.00-20.00.* Garden, children and dogs welcome. Camping. *Open daily 12.00-22.00.*

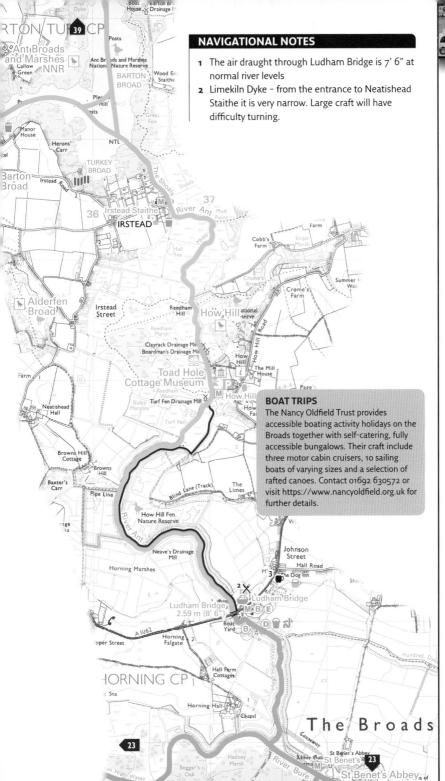

NAVIGATIONAL NOTES

1. The air draught through Ludham Bridge is 7' 6" at normal river levels
2. Limekiln Dyke – from the entrance to Neatishead Staithe it is very narrow. Large craft will have difficulty turning.

BOAT TRIPS

The Nancy Oldfield Trust provides accessible boating activity holidays on the Broads together with self-catering, fully accessible bungalows. Their craft include three motor cabin cruisers, 10 sailing boats of varying sizes and a selection of rafted canoes. Contact 01692 630572 or visit https://www.nancyoldfield.org.uk for further details.

Hickling

The passage across the great expanse of Hickling Broad is extremely pleasurable and above the reed-fringed edges often as many as five wind pumps can be seen beneath towering skies. On leaving the broad, the thatched Royal Shooting Lodge is passed at White Slea. The channel narrows through Depp-Go Dyke, then spreads out into Heigham Sound. To the north east is Meadow Dyke, an intimate channel through extensive reed beds. If you are lucky you may see them being cut and stacked by hand, and then taken out by punt. Then suddenly you are on the remote and lovely Horsey Mere. Waxham New Cut, a narrow cul-de-sac, heads off north; in the east is Horsey Mill, while it is an easy 30-minute walk to the sea from here.

● **Hickling**
Norfolk. PO box. A popular if undistinguished Broads village, handy for both the coast and for inland boating. Standing alone in a field is the tall, sail-less Grade II* Hickling Mill, with recently restored cap, while to the north east are the scant remains of an Augustinian priory, founded in 1185. **Hickling Broad and Marshes** Norfolk Wildlife Trust https://www.norfolkwildlifetrust.org.uk/wildlife-in-norfolk/nature-reserves/reserves/hickling-broad-and-marshes. A 1360-acre site of astonishing beauty originally acquired by the NNT in 1945 – the largest of the Broads. Reed and sedge beds, oak woodlands and wader scrapes (artificial ponds) attract a wide variety of birdlife, including such unlikely migrants as ospreys, spoonbills and avocets. In May and June you may possibly see colourful swallowtail butterflies. Famous for its large pike and shoals of bream, the Broad has in the past suffered from outbreaks of the alga prymnesium and many fish have died. It has, however, been restocked. There are various nature trials, mostly wheelchair-friendly, boardwalks and bird-watching hides. Visitor Centre with interpretive boards, café and toilets.

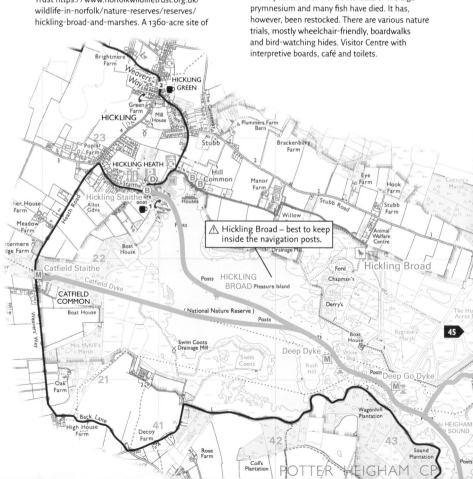

⚠ Hickling Broad – best to keep inside the navigation posts.

Pubs and Restaurants (pages 42–45)

◉ **1 The Pleasure Boat Inn** Staithe Road, Hickling NR12 0YW (01692 598870; www.ThePleasureboat. com). Attractive waterside pub with attached café (*open daily 10.00–16.00*) a microbrewery and a shop selling non-perishables for boaters. Pub *open all year* serving a range of real ales and ciders, including beers from their own brewery. Food available *Mon–Fri L and E & Sat–Sun all day*. Large waterside garden. Mooring. *Open 11.30–23.00 (Sun 12.00).*

◉✕ **2 The Greyhound Inn** The Green, Hickling NR12 0YA (01692 598306; www.greyhoundinn.com). Friendly, family-run village pub, serving real ales and good pub food available *daily L and E*. Attractive garden and outside eating area, dog-friendly. Traditional pub games, real fires and Wi-Fi. Camping nearby. *Open 12.00–23.00.*

◉✕ **3 The Nelson Head** The Street, Horsey NR29 4AD (01493 393378; www.thenelsonhead. com). Real ales and real cider together with traditional pub fare served *Mon–Fri L and E & Sat–Sun 12.00–21.00 (Sun 20.00)* in a friendly, welcoming local, close to the sea. Garden, dog- and child-friendly. Traditional pub games, real fires and Wi-Fi. Mooring. *Open 11.00–23.00.*

✕♗ **4 Poppylands** Waxham Road, Horsey NR29 4EQ (01493 393393). Located a short distance north of Horsey windpump and the village of Horsey. Poppylands is a traditional 1940s café, with many period artefacts, serving a wide range of traditional favourites including Bubble and Squeak, Bangers and Mash and Spam Fritters. Lunches and freshly-baked cream teas served to the sound of Vera Lynn, Glen Miller and the Andrews Sisters. Dog-friendly. *Open daily 10.00–15.30.*

NAVIGATIONAL NOTES

In Hickling Broad and Heigham Sound keep to the marked channel between the posts.

BOAT TRIPS

The *Electric Eel* – an Edwardian-style electric boat – takes you through quiet backwaters with breathtaking views of the Broads. It runs *May to Sep* (weather permitting) and takes you by boat across open water, through reeds to the base of the Tree Tower, and is an excellent way to explore How Hill Nature Reserve. From the top of the Tower there is an amazing view of the Broads and coast. The Tree Tower is accessible only on the Water Trail (01603 756096; www.visitnorfolk.co.uk/ The-Broads-Wildlife-Water-Trail/details/?dms=3&venue=0210617).

Ross' wildlife boat trips on the Lady Ann are based on Horsey Mere and depart from Horsey Staithe NR29 4EF. The Lady Ann is a classic wooden boat, stable and perfect for viewing the unique wildlife of the Mere's SSSI. For further details contact 07791 526440 or visit www.nationaltrust.org. uk/horsey-windpump/features/ross-wildlife-boat-trips-at-horsey-windpump. Well-behaved dogs welcome.

The *Norfolk Wildlife Trust* (www.norfolkwildlifetrust.org.uk/wildlife-in-norfolk/nature-reserves/ facilities/boat-trips) operate guided electric boat trips on Ranworth and Hickling Broads throughout the season. Visit their website for further details.

Horsey

Norfolk. A remote settlement described in 1842 as 'a most desolate place' when it was inhabited by marshmen and wildfowlers. All Saints church has a round tower (of 180 such round towers in England, almost 120 are in Norfolk) and bench ends carved with poppy heads. A mile to the east, past the pub, is the seashore which can also be accessed at Horsey Gap (NR29 4EJ) by following the road north east past Poppylands. It was near here in 1287 that a disastrous storm broke through the sea defences causing severe flooding and damaging, amongst other buildings, St Benet's Abbey, Horning. More recent floods occurred in 1938 when half a mile of dunes were lost and 7000 acres flooded, and in 1953, when the sea broke through at Sea Palling. Swimming in the sea here is not recommended.

Horsey Mere National Trust. A slightly brackish but very attractive expanse of water, rich in ducks, waders and geese. The entrance to the narrow Waxham cut is to be found in the north west corner.

Horsey Windpump Horsey, NR29 4EE (01263 740241). A four-storey red-brick wind pump, built on the foundations of an old mill in 1912 and now owned by the National Trust. This windpump has a dramatic history having survived floods, a lightning strike, collapse, storms and gale-force winds. Located in a great area for birdwatching, overlooking Horsey Mere – also managed by the National Trust – it enjoys fine views across the Broads. Nature garden, including raised ponds and a wildflower meadow. Shop and tearoom *open daily 11.00-16.00.*

Waxham Great Barn Sea Palling NR12 0DZ (01603 629048; www.nhbt.org.uk/properties/ waxham-great-barn-grade-i). A Grade I listed barn, originally constructed in the late 16th C, with later additions. Much of the building material was reused from dissolved monasteries. At 180ft in length, it is the largest barn in Norfolk. Café. *Open Apr-Oct, 09.00-17.00. Telephone or visit website to confirm times.* Charge.

Thurne Dyke

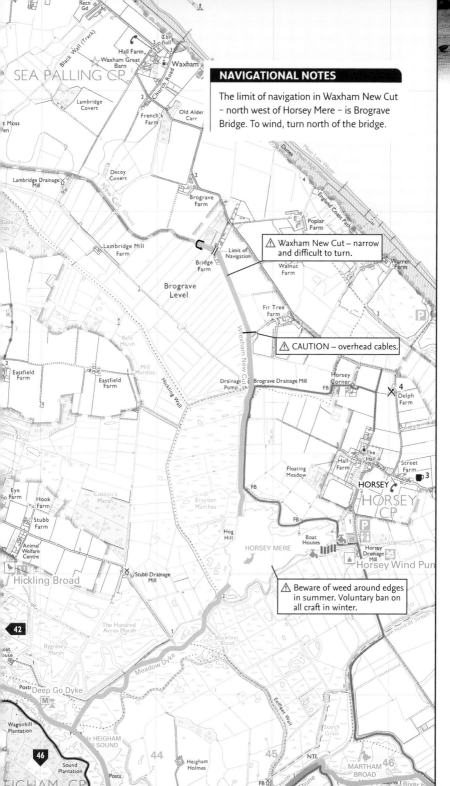

NAVIGATIONAL NOTES

The limit of navigation in Waxham New Cut – north west of Horsey Mere – is Brograve Bridge. To wind, turn north of the bridge.

⚠ Waxham New Cut – narrow and difficult to turn.

⚠ CAUTION – overhead cables.

⚠ Beware of weed around edges in summer. Voluntary ban on all craft in winter.

SEA PALLING CP

Recn Gd

The Hall

Hall Farm,
Waxham Great Barn

Waxham

Black Wall (Track)

Church Road

Lambridge Covert

French's Farm

Old Alder Carr

t Moss en

Decoy Covert

Lambridge Drainage Mill

New Cut (Drain)

Brograve Farm

Mean Low Water

Dunes

England Coast Path

Poplar Farm

Lambridge Mill Farm

Bridge Farm

Limit of Navigation

Walnut Farm

Warren Farm

Brograve Level

Fir Tree Farm

P

Bells Marsh

Mill Marshes

Hickling Wall

Waxham New Cut

Eastfield Farm

Eastfield Farm

Drainage Pump

Brograve Drainage Mill

FB

Horsey Corner

X 4 Delph Farm

oners Drain

Eye Farm

Hook Farm

Cotton's Marsh

Floating Meadow

Hall Farm

Street Farm

3

HORSEY

Stubb Farm

Brayden Marshes

FB

HORSEY CP

Animal Welfare Centre

FB

Hickling Broad

Stubb Drainage Mill

Hog Hill

HORSEY MERE

Boat Houses

1

P

M

Horsey Drainage Mill

Horsey Wind Pu

42

The Hundred Acres Marsh

Blackfleet Broad

Hundred Stream

Bygrave Marsh

Meadow Dyke

Post
Deep Go Dyke

M

Wagonhill Plantation

46

Sound Plantation

EIGHAM CP

LE HEIGHAM SOUND

44

Heigham Holmes

45

Eelfleet Wall

Starch Grass

NTL

MARTHAM BROAD

46

River Thurne

FB

West Somerton

As the River Thurne leaves West Somerton its slightly elevated position offers splendid views over rich farmland. Horsey Mill to the north and the Caistor Water Tower to the south are easily identified landmarks. After Martham Broad, the Hundred Stream joins amidst vast reed beds and the main river heads south west to Martham Ferry where there are some summer chalets and moored craft around the rather unusual floating swing bridge which was constructed in 2012 to access Heigham Holmes.

● West Somerton
Norfolk. PO box. The thatched church of St Mary stands to the east of this small rambling village. Its Norman round tower has an octagonal belfry; inside there are 14th-C wall paintings depicting Christ on a rainbow together with St Christopher, now rather faded. Look for the funny faces on the pulpit and the 15th-C backless bench in the airy chapel. In the graveyard lies Robert Hales, the Somerton Giant, who was 7' 8" tall and weight 33 stone. He died, aged 50, in 1863. Somerton Hall stands by the church; in the grounds there was once a leper hospital owned by Bentley Priory in Suffolk.

● Winterton-on-Sea
Norfolk. PO, stores, off-licence, fish & chips. One and a half miles to the east of West Somerton and a very pleasant walk. A charming little town with narrow streets, very much like the Yarmouth 'Rows', which has now succumbed to the holiday trade. To the north is Winterton Dunes – 260 acres of heath, bog and dune.

● Martham
Norfolk. PO, stores, off-licence, chemist, takeaways, fish & chips, library. There are some fine Georgian houses around two large greens in this village which lies a mile to the south of the Norfolk Wildlife Trust nature reserve of Martham Broad. St Mary's church has a massive west tower culminating in a spike. Beneath this edifice is a stone to Alice Burraway, put in place by her husband, which recalls that 'in this life (she was) my sister, my mistress, my mother and my wife'. He was born as a result of an incestuous union between his father and his sister. Unknowingly, following an affair, he later married Alice.

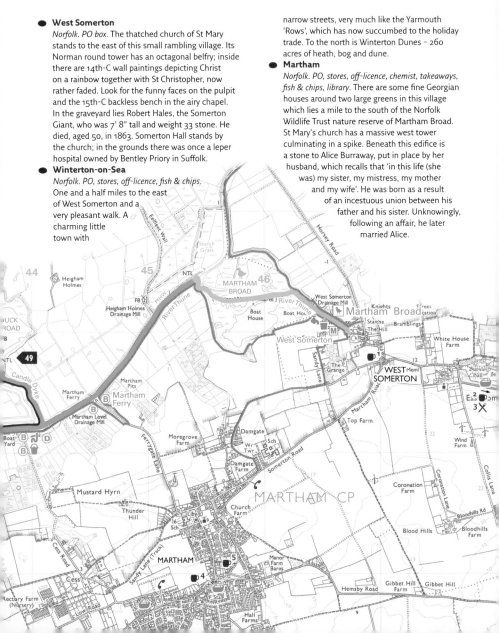

THE SECRET AIRFIELD

Conflicting stories surround the wartime use of Heigham Holmes, a 500-acre island in the marshes and now manged by the National Trust for wildlife and grazing. Local legend has it that it was used as a forward landing strip, by the black-painted Lysanders of 161 Squadron for the SOE, parachuting agents into occupied Holland. It was reputed to be chosen for its remoteness and the RAF staff were billeted in the single farmhouse. The only other two dwellings housed marshmen whose duties included cleaning out ditches and tending windpumps. In contrast to all this purported activity, their lives were 'insular' to say the least: one of the wives never left the island, merely walking down to the ferry on a weekly basis to buy provision from a trading wherry.

There is even uncertainty over the precise location of the landing strip, with 1943 aerial photographs showing it on the east side of the farmhouse and the Scheduled Monument Register delignating it on the western boundary. What can be deduced is that few agents survived in the Low Countries for very long, due to the Derricourt and Buckmaster Doublecross, members of the Prospero Ring.

But in terms of certainty, we can be absolutely sure that documentary evidence was either destroyed at the end of hostilities or embargoed for 100 years due to the secret nature of these operations. It will therefore be 2045 when the true wartime use of Heigham Holmes will finally be revealed.

Pubs and Restaurants

⬛✗ 1 The Lion Staithe Road, West Somerton NR29 4DP (01493 393861; www.thelionsomerton. co.uk). Warm and welcoming, serving excellent home-cooked food made from local ingredients, together with real ales. Food available *Tue-Fri (not Tue L) & Sat-Sun 12.00-21.00 (Sun 19.00)*. Garden, dog- and family-friendly. Traditional pub games and Wi-Fi. B&B. Mooring nearby. *Open Tue E & Wed-Sun 12.00-23.00 (Sun 22.30)*.

⬛✗ 2 The Fisherman's Return The Lane, Winterton-on-Sea NR29 4BN (01493 393305; www.fishermansreturn.com). Welcoming 17th-C pub, within easy reach of the sea, featuring a traditional Norfolk brick and flint exterior. Real ale, real cider and an appetising range of home-cooked food is served *L and E*. Outside seating, dog- and family-friendly. Traditional pub games, real fires and Wi-Fi. B&B. *Open Mon-Sat 11.00-23.00 (out of season Mon-Fri L and E) & Sun 12.00-22.30*.

✗ 3 Poppy's at Winterton on Sea Beach Road, Winterton-on-Sea NR29 4AJ (01493 393238; www. facebook.com/PoppysAtWintertonOnSea). Dog-friendly tearoom, *open Mon-Sat 08.30-16.30 & Sun 08.30* (call to book). Afternoon teas should be *pre-ordered the day before.*

⬛ 4 The Victory Inn 12 Repps Road, Martham NR29 4QT (01493 740774; www.facebook.com/ Victoria-Inn-160751753939663). Friendly two-bar local dispensing real ale and *occasional* live music. Outside seating, dog-friendly. Sports TV and Wi-Fi. *Open 12.00-23.00 (Sun 22.30)*.

⬛✗ 5 The Kings Arms 15 The Green, Martham NR29 4PL (01493 749156; www.facebook.com/ thekingsarmsmarthamthem). A friendly pub in the heart of the settlement, overlooking the village pond, serving a range of real ales and ciders. Home-cooked food available *Tue-Sun 12.00-21.00 (Sun 18.00)*. Garden and play area, dog- and child-friendly. Children in restaurant and garden only *after 18.00*. Real fires and Wi-Fi. *Open Tue-Sun 12.00-22.30 (Fri-Sat 23.00) & B Hol Mon all day.*

Potter Heigham

The approach to Potter Heigham is marked by ever increasing numbers of summer houses and chalets of indiscriminate vintage. Many are quite attractive and virtually all have their own off-line mooring. After the low New Bridge comes the tiny arch of the old, where bridge pilots squeeze large craft through at high speed, while lesser mortals and landlubbers look on. Now there are even more summer houses, over a mile of then on both sides, before the river is once again in open country. A diversion to Ludham along Womack Water is most rewarding. Over its short length is a microcosm of Broadland scenery, with the chance of seeing the sailing wherry *Albion*, moored at Forsythe Wherry Yard. Continuing south the River Thurne passes the village that is its namesake, the entrance to the dyke is marked by a very handsome white windpump.

● Potter Heigham
Norfolk. PO, stores, off-licence, fish & chips, DIY, hardware, takeaways. The discovery of wood ash from the kilns of a Roman pottery reveal the origins of this unusually named village, the true centre of which is a mile north west of the holiday centre which has burgeoned around the medieval bridge. This 1385 bridge, with its notoriously low and narrow arch, is such an obstacle that hire companies operate a pilot service to help their unwary holiday makers through. The church of St Nicholas dates from 13th C and has a round tower topped with a 15th-C belfry. Its hammer-beam roof is particularly handsome.

High's Mill A riverside, red-brick tower mill, above Potter Heigham, complete with boat-shaped cap and now converted into a private dwelling.

● Ludham
Norfolk. Stores, butcher, garage. An attractive village with some good houses and a large 14th-C church. Dedicated to St Catherine, who was put to death on a spiked wheel, her emblem has been incorporated into the roof. The font is decorated with wild men and lions; the screen painted with 11 saints and a king. There is also a fine 15th-C painting of the crucifixion and a large poor box of a similar age.

Wherry *Albion* Norfolk Wherry Trust Forsythe Wherry Yard, Horsefen Road, Ludham NR29 5QG (01362 822058/07586 353904; www.wherryalbion. com). For many years the only surviving trading wherry on the Broads, since joined by *Maud* – rebuilt at Upton – and six other examples, a total of seven being on the National Register of Historic Ships. Interestingly, *Albion* was one of the few such craft to be carvel-built (i.e. having the planking joined flush at the seams) the great majority being clinker-built (i.e. having

the planks overlapping at the seams). Five of the eight wherries are looked after by the Wherry Yacht Charter Charitable Trust The Wherry Base, Barton House, Hartwell Road, Wroxham NR12 8TL (01603 781475; www.wherryyachtcharter. org) and can be chartered. *Day* trips are also available.

Toad Hole Cottage Museum Ludham, NR29 5PG (01603 756096/678763). This tiny marshman's cottage on the River Ant was home for a whole family in Victorian times. You can visit the cottage to see how they lived and the tools they used for working on the marshes. Also watch a video and read about how Toad Hole was rethatched in March 2017. The cottage also has information and displays about How Hill and the Broads and tickets can be bought for the wildlife walking trail. The Electric Eel boat trip offers you the chance to explore along dykes fringed with marshland plants and an experienced guide will show you the wildlife

WALKING AND CYCLING
The Weavers Way is a 29-mile cross-country walk from Cromer to Stalham, through what was once the heart of the Norfolk weaving trade. Between Heigham Bridge and Thurne it follows the south bank of the river.

BOAT TRIPS
See Norfolk Wherry Trust opposite, page 49

including dragonflies, marsh harriers, wildflowers and swallowtail butterflies.

- **Thurne**
  Norfolk. PO box. An unspoilt village just north of the confluence of the Rivers Thurne and Bure. The church of St Edmund dates from 14thC. A tiny window in the crenellated tower looks out towards St Benet's Abbey – it is said that a lamp placed here could signal a warning to the monks at the Abbey. There is a parish slipway for hire at £5 per launch or recovery – The Street, Thurne NR29 3BU.

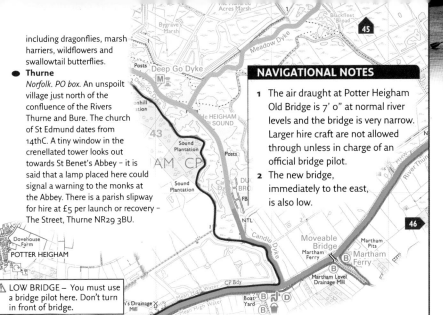

⚠ LOW BRIDGE – You must use a bridge pilot here. Don't turn in front of bridge.

Potter Heigham Bridge Green

Potter Heigham New Bridge 2.31 m (7' 7")
Old Bridge 1.98 m (6' 6")

Potter Heigham

Martham Bank

Bastwick

Epps

Norfolk Wherry Trust

Forsythe Wherry Yard, Horsefen Road, Ludham NR29 5QG (https://www.wherryalbion.com). Saviours of the Wherry *Albion*, a 123-year-old traditional Norfolk Wherry. Known as a 'black sailed trader', she is one of only two remaining commercial Wherries built specifically for the Broads. At their peak there were over 300 of these craft, but now *Albion* is one of only a very few available for hire. In the *summer months* during the Edwardian era, skippers scrubbed out the holds and took holiday makers for trips to make extra money. To follow in Edwardian footsteps, and explore the unique Broads wetlands beneath *Albion's* vast black sail, there are *open days* (telephone or visit website) and charter opportunities.

Thurne Dyke Drainage Pump A very pretty and distinctive white-painted tower built by England's of Ludham in 1820 and now in private ownership. Another handsome windpump stands on the opposite bank.

Thurne Wind Pump Marsh Road, Repps With Bastwick, Great Yarmouth NR29 5JU (07796 407864; https://www.thurnewindmill.co.uk). When 'Bob' Morse initially bought the mill, from the Internal Drainage Board in 1949, it was in extremely poor

condition and had, in fact, ceased working in 1936. The internal floors, doors and windows had gone. The sails and fantail needed replacement and the brickwork required immediate attention. Bob wasted no time and began work straight away. He hired Albert England, a direct descendant of the millwright Dan England of Ludham, who had built the mill in 1820. Between them they repaired and re-painted the tower restoring it as one of the most iconic mills on the Norfolk Broads.

Wind Energy Museum Staithe Road, Repps with Bastwick, Great Yarmouth NR29 5JU (07796 407864; www.windenergymuseum.co.uk). Featuring full sized wind pumps, steam engines and a unique scoop wheel along with photographs, models of mills, stories and working examples that depict the evolution of drainage on the Broads. Due to the broad collection of exhibits and activities, the Museum holds interest for all age groups. The majority of the mills featured at the Museum are some of the last remaining examples of their kind in the UK. Guided tours of the Museum add an extra touch to the visit. Shop. *Regular open days –* telephone or visit website for details.

NAVIGATIONAL NOTES

1. The air draught at Potter Heigham Old Bridge is 7' 0" at normal river levels and the bridge is very narrow. Larger hire craft are not allowed through unless in charge of an official bridge pilot.
2. The new bridge, immediately to the east, is also low.

Pubs and Restaurants

🚤✗ **1 The Falgate Inn** Ludham Road, Potter Heigham NR29 5HZ (01692 670003). 18th-C hostelry with oak beams and an open fire. Good value pub food served in an extended restaurant area. Booking essential on boat change over days. Garden. B&B.

🚤 **2 The Kings Arms** High Street, Ludham NR29 5QQ (01692 678386; www.kingsarmsludham.co.uk). Significantly extended pub in the middle of the village, serving real ales and food *daily 12.00-21.00* including a carvery *Wed & Sun*. Live music *most Fri*. Pool table and sports TV.

THE RIVER YARE

The Broads Authority publish guidance to the River Yare and the River Wensum at www.broads-authority.gov.uk/boating/navigating-the-broads/water-depths/river-yare which includes further helpful tips and can be read in conjunction with this guide. These are particularly useful for water depth, speed limits and channel details which can alter regularly due to bank works and tidal movement.

Rising south of Shipdham in Norfolk, the Yare has long been navigable from Norwich to Great Yarmouth where it joins the River Bure below the shallow, tidal expanse of Breydon Water, to pass through Yarmouth Harbour to the sea. Indeed, it was this lack of depth in Breydon Water which necessitated the transhipment of goods from sea-going vessels to smaller craft able to make the passage to Norwich, thus giving Yarmouth a stranglehold on all trade going inland. The Norwich merchants were anxious to free themselves from this obstacle and various schemes were mooted to improve the river, all to be blocked in one way or another by the men of Yarmouth, who obviously recognised a good thing when they saw it.

Finally, in 1827, after giving much evidence of malpractice at Yarmouth, Norwich finally got a bill through Parliament enabling them to improve the navigation and bypass Yarmouth by building the Haddiscoe New Cut and opening Oulton Broad and Lake Lothing to the sea at Lowestoft. The improved 32-mile navigation, which enabled sea-going vessels to reach Norwich, was officially opened in 1833.

Unfortunately, receipts were not sufficient to recover the investment and, to add to the difficulties, Lake Lothing silted up. Railway building did not improve matters either. By 1850 the traffic was once again passing through Yarmouth, with the New Cut little used. Until fairly recently small coasters used to make the journey up river to Norwich (via Yarmouth) mooring in the town centre on the River Wensum.

Mooring on the River Wensum in Norwich

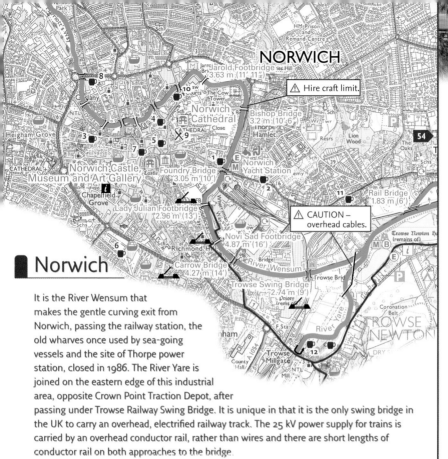

Norwich

It is the River Wensum that makes the gentle curving exit from Norwich, passing the railway station, the old wharves once used by sea-going vessels and the site of Thorpe power station, closed in 1986. The River Yare is joined on the eastern edge of this industrial area, opposite Crown Point Traction Depot, after passing under Trowse Railway Swing Bridge. It is unique in that it is the only swing bridge in the UK to carry an overhead, electrified railway track. The 25 kV power supply for trains is carried by an overhead conductor rail, rather than wires and there are short lengths of conductor rail on both approaches to the bridge.

● **Norwich**
Norfolk. All services. The county town, social capital and market centre of Norfolk. Its irregular street plan indicates Saxon origins, while a wealth of surviving buildings testifies to its continued importance from the early Middle Ages onwards. In addition to its magnificent cathedral, Norwich could once boast a church for every Sunday in the year and a pub for every other day of the year. The Industrial Revolution, which dealt the final blow to its hand-weaving industry, saw the birth of the city as one of the chief shoe manufacturing towns in the country. The city centre is enclosed on three sides by the old city wall, the curve of the River Wensum defining the fourth. Modern development has been judiciously restrained (with a few exceptions) and many of the city's old buildings have been saved and restored. With its twisting streets and alleys, glimpses of the great castle keep or the cathedral spire around virtually every corner, and a bustling market at its heart, Norwich is the ideal town to explore on foot.

Norwich Castle From its high mound the castle dominates the city centre. The magnificent keep was built in 12th C but owes its pristine condition to refacing in 19th C. It had a turbulent early history

and was made into the city goal in 1220, a function it retained until 1887 when it was converted into the county museum and art gallery. Although the museum has subsequently been modernised, the Great Hall on the first floor remains much as it must have been 600 years ago. Of major interest are the fine natural history galleries and a comprehensive collection of paintings of the Norwich School, as well as archaeological exhibits, Lowestoft porcelain and Norwich silver. There are also galleries devoted to Boudicca, Queen of the Iceni, Anglo-Saxons and Vikings. Step even further back in time to experience the atmosphere of an Egyptian tomb with its ancient mummies. There are *regular* conducted tours of the battlements and castle dungeons. Shop and café. Charge.

Norwich Cathedral This beautiful example of Norman architecture was begun in 1096 by Herbert de Losinga on the Pope's orders, as a punishment for the sin of simony. Herbert certainly paid his penance well!

The splendid vaulted roof of the nave has over 300 carved bosses and there are more in the cloisters, totalling 1200 in all. It is thought that Bishop's Throne, behind the altar, may be 1000 years old, which make it the oldest in any English cathedral. The graceful, splendid spire is second in height only to that at Salisbury, and is equally lovely. It's a 15th-C replacement of an earlier spire which collapsed in 1362. The cathedral close stretches down to the River Wensum and the 15th-C river gate, Pull's Ferry. There are a number of excellent Georgian buildings in the close.

The two cathedral gates face the cobbled square of Tombland. The Erpingham Gate is regarded as one of the finest in the Perpendicular style. St Ethelbert's is slightly earlier, built jointly by the townspeople and monks as a penance after one of their periodic riots in the Middle Ages.

Bridewell Museum Bridewell Alley, Norwich NR2 1AQ (01603 629127; https://www.museums.norfolk.gov.uk/museum-of-norwich). Built upon a vaulted 14th-C undercroft, Norwich's main museum has exhibits relating to local crafts and industries from the Middle Ages to the present day. A fascinating and wide-ranging collection. *Opening times* vary so telephone or visit the website.

Elm Hill Norwich NH3 1HG. 200yds west of the cathedral. This is one of the most picturesque streets in the city. Pastel-painted red-brick and irregular timber buildings shoulder to shoulder along a narrow cobbled street. Lantern-lit by night. Named after the elm trees that stood here in Henry VIII's reign.

Maddermarket Theatre St Johns Alley, Norwich NR2 1DR (01603 620917; www.maddermarket.co.uk). The Maddermarket Theatre is a recreation of an Elizabethan Theatre. It opened in 1921 as a result of the leadership of Nugent Monck, who founded the Norwich Players who perform regularly in the venue, alongside visiting theatrical productions and the Norwich Jazz club. Box office *open Mon-Fri 10.00-17.00 & Sat 10.00-13.00*.

Norwich Arts Centre Reeves Yard, St Benedict's Street, Norwich NR2 4PG (01603 660352; www.norwichartscentre.co.uk). Norwich Arts Centre, housed in the converted 14th-C church of St Swithun, has a lively programme of exhibitions and family events, but is also distinguished by a commitment to live performance, featuring touring bands and live comedy.

Norwich Castle Museum & Art Gallery 24 Castle Meadow, Norwich NR1 3JU (01603493625; www.museums.norfolk.gov.uk/norwich-castle). Housing excellent galleries of archaeology, natural and regimental history. Decorative and contemporary art. Also a changing exhibition programme and interpretation built around the castle's history. *Opening times vary* so telephone or visit the website.

Norwich Cathedral The Close, Norwich NR1 4DH (01603 218300; www.cathedral.org.uk). Founded in 1096 and built in the Romanesque style. It has been voted Norfolk's most loved building. The cathedral has the second tallest spire and the largest monastic cloisters in England, much of the building retaining its

medieval splendour. The herb garden is a pleasant retreat. Restaurant/coffee shop. Cathedral *open daily 07.30-18.00*. Restaurant *open daily 10.00-17.00 (Sun 11.00)*. Garden *open daily 09.00-17.00*. Shop *open Mon-Sat 09.15 17.00 & Sun 11.45-15.30*.

Norwich Playhouse 42–58 St George's Street, Norwich NR3 1AB (01603 598598; www.norwichplayhouse.co.uk). A 300-seat riverside theatre developed from a Georgian maltings. The programme spans theatre, stand up comedy, live music and children's shows. The building includes two galleries exhibiting work by local artists, a bar and a garden.

Norwich Puppet Theatre St James, Whitefriars, Norwich NR3 1TN (01603629921; www.puppettheatre.co.uk). Norwich Puppet Theatre is one of two dedicated puppet theatres in England. It opened in 1980 in the purpose converted medieval church of St James. The theatre offers a year-round programme of family-centred entertainment and acts as a centre of excellence for all things puppetry. *Open Mon-Fri 09.30-17.30 & Sat 09.30-17.00 on performance days*.

St Peter Mancroft Hay Hill, Norwich NR2 1QQ (01603 610443; www.stpetermancroft.org.uk). This 15th-C church stands in splendour above the Market Place, with a lavishly panelled and substantial tower arched over the street. It is crowned by turrets and a charming Victorian Gothic spirelet, and a little lost in the midst of such a spectacle. The clerestory forms a magnificent wall of light in the lofty interior, meeting the boss-studded roof in which the hammer-beams are covered by coving. A fine panoply of 15th-C stained glass fills the east window. Also of note are the impressive canopy over the font and the brasses and monuments. *Open Mon-Fri 12.30-13.30 & Sat 12.00-14.00*.

Sewell Barn Theatre Constitution Hill, Norwich NR3 4BB (01603 626414; www.sewellbarn.org). Home to a popular amateur theatre company, with close historical links to the author Anna Sewell who wrote Black Beauty. For tickets telephone 01603 626414 *Mon-Sat 09.30-17.30*.

Stranger's Hall 4 Charing Cross, Norwich NR2 4AL (01603 493625; www.museums.norfolk.gov.uk/strangers-hall). A 15th-C merchant's house, Grade I listed, built upon an earlier late 13th-C undercroft. Its name derives from immigrant cloth-workers who lived here in the 17th C. Furnished rooms show a variety of fashions between 16th and 19th C and it now houses a museum of costumes and period furniture. *Opening times vary* so telephone or visit the website.

Tourist Information Centre (www.visitnorwich.co.uk). Online service only.

NAVIGATIONAL NOTES

1 The navigational limit for hire craft is Bishopgate Bridge, immediately above the Yacht Station. Small craft can navigate further upstream as far as the sluices at New Mills Yard.

2 Navigation on the River Yare, upstream of its confluence with the Wensum to Trowse Millgate, is not recommended as the river is narrow and there is little space to turn.

3 There is a low overhead cable on the River Yare approximately ¼ mile upstream of its confluence with the Wensum.

🍺 1 The Compleat Angler 120 Prince of Wales Road, Norwich NR1 1NS (01603 622425; www.greeneking-pubs.co.uk/pubs/norfolk/compleat-angler). Large pub, handy for the railway station and Yacht Station, with a pretty riverside terrace, dispensing real ales and food *daily 11.00-23.00 (Sun 22.00)*. Garden, dogs welcome. Sports TV and Wi-Fi. Mooring. *Open 11.00-00.00 (Sun 22.30)*.

🍺 2 The King's Head 42 Magdalen Street, Norwich NR3 1JE (01603 620468; www.facebook.com/kingsheadnorwich). A very serious real ale pub, majoring on Norfolk beers and ciders; bar snacks available and cutlery etc. provided for those bringing in food from local takeaways. Outside, cobbled area; dogs welcome. Traditional pub games, newspapers and Wi-Fi. *Open daily 12.00-00.00*.

🍺 3 The Plough 58 St Benedict Street, Norwich NR2 4AR (01603 661384; www.instagram.com/ploughnorwich). Stylish, brewery tap, serving Grain Brewery real ales and the occasional guest; also cocktails. Vicky's special sausage pie *always* available. *Summer* barbeques. Large Mediterranean-style courtyard, dogs welcome. Newspapers, real fires and Wi-Fi. *Open Mon-Sat 12.00-23.00 (Fri-Sat 00.00) & Sun 12.00-22.30*.

🍺 4 The Ribs of Beef 24 Wensum Street, Norwich NR3 1HY (01603 619517; www.ribsofbeef.co.uk). Standing beside the ancient Fye Bridge, this traditional town pub dispenses an excellent selection of real ales, real cider and food, made from locally-sourced ingredients, *daily 12.00-21.00 (Sun 17.00)*. Terrace, dogs (on a lead) welcome. *Sun* live music. Newspapers, sports TV and Wi-Fi. Mooring. *Open 11.00-23.00 (Fri-Sat 00.00) & Sun 11.00-22.00*.

🍺 5 Louise Marchesi 17 Tombland, Norwich NR3 1HF (01603 763099; www.louismarchesi.co.uk). A Grade II listed, timber-framed building, parts of which date from 15th C, dispensing real ales and real ciders. Good choice of wines, gins, cocktails and whiskies. Food is available *L and E (not Mon L or Sun E)*. Tiny, enclosed patio; dogs welcome. Newspapers, real fires and Wi-Fi. *Open Mon 17.00-23.00; Tue-Sat 11.00-23.00 (Fri-Sat 00.01) & Sun 12.00-22.30*.

🍺 6 The Trafford Arms 61 Grove Road, Norwich NR1 3RL (01603 628466; www.traffordarms.co.uk). Popular, award-winning, community local, dispensing a wide range of real ales and food *Mon-Sat L and E & Sun 10.00-18.00*. Outside seating, family-friendly. Newspapers, sports TV and Wi-Fi. *Open Mon-Fri 11.00-23.00 (Fri 23.30) & Sat-Sun 10.00-23.30 (Sun 22.30)*.

🍺✕ 7 The Vine 7 Dove Street, Norwich NR2 1DE (01603 627362; www.vinethai.co.uk). Reputed to be the smallest pub in Norwich, this wee hostelry punches way above its weight, dispensing real ales, real ciders and appetising Thai cuisine *Mon-Sat L and E*. Vegetarians and vegans catered for. Outside seating. Traditional pub games. *Open Mon-Sat 11.00-23.00*.

🍺 8 The White Lion 73 Oak Street, Norwich NR3 3AQ (01603 632333; www.facebook.com/WhiteLionNorwich). The only remaining hostelry in a street that once boasted 31, this comfortable pub majors on ciders and perries, alongside a good choice of real ales. Food is available *Wed-Thu E & Fri-Sun L and E (not Sun E)*. Outside seating, dogs welcome. Traditional pub games, real fires and Wi-Fi. *Open Mon-Sat 12.00-23.00 (Fri-Sat 23.30) & Sun 12.00-22.30*.

✕🍷 9 The Giggling Squid 24 Tombland, Norwich NR3 1RF (01603 667341; https://www.gigglingsquid.com/restaurant/norwich). Set in a lovely large Grade II listed building, with stained glass windows, this welcoming establishment veers towards the whimsical, whilst serving appetising food (including vegan options) *daily 12.00-22.00 (Sun 21.30)*.

🍺✕ 10 The Wig & Pen 6 St Martin-At-Palace Plain, Norwich NR3 1RN (01603 625891; www.thewigandpen.com). City-centre pub, with a friendly 'local' feel, set in a 17th-C building – exposed brickwork, wooden beams and all. Also real ales and excellent food available *Sun-Thu L and E (not Sun E) & Fri-Sat 11.30-21.00*. Outside seating. Sports TV and Wi-Fi. B&B. *Open Mon-Sat 11.30-23.00 (Fri-Sat 00.00) & Sun 11.30-18.30*.

🍺 11 The Fat Cat & Canary 101 Thorpe Road, Norwich NR1 1TR (01603 436393; www.facebook.com/fatcatcanary). One third of a mile west of Thorpe Green moorings. Shrugging off its earlier connections with the old Colman's mustard steam tug, this pub now dispenses most of the local Fat Cat Brewery ales, together with brews (including cider) from further afield. Homemade rolls generally available with home-cooked meals *Sun 12.00-17.00 (and most Fri E)*. Patio seating, dog- and child-friendly. Sports TV and Wi-Fi. *Open Sun-Fri 12.00-23.00 (Fri 00.00) & Sat 11.00-00.00*.

🍺 12 The White Horse Inn The Street, Trowse NR14 8ST (01603 622341; www.whitehorsetrowse.co.uk). Overlooking the village green (complete with children's playground) this food-oriented pub serves real ales, a good selection of malt whiskies and meals *L and E (not Sun-Mon E)*. Folk club *Fri* and *regular* karaoke. Patio seating. Pub shop selling bedding plants, compost and the like. Real fires and Wi-Fi. *Open daily 11.30-23.00*.

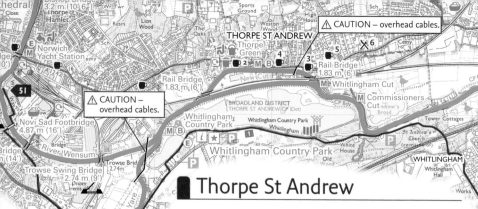

Thorpe St Andrew

The New Cut offers the most direct route for those not wishing
to visit Thorpe St Andrew. The course of the river is wide and
deep as you might expect on a navigation that once was home to
coasters looming unexpectedly around the many blind bends.
Fortunately for today's boater this trade ceased some 40 years ago! Attractive
woodlands flank the south bank at Whitlingham, followed by Whitlingham Marsh and gently
undulating farmland to the north. The pretty Bramerton Woods contrast starkly with Postwick
Marsh before the Ferry House pub at Surlingham is reached. Both banks are thickly wooded below
this point.

● **Trowse**

Norfolk PO, stores, off-licence, takeaway. Trowse
(or Trowse with Newton to give the village its full
appellation) derives from the word 'trouse' which
is a grating that can be lifted or lowered to control
the flow of water, in this case to the mill race of the
local flour mill at Trowse Millgate. It was expanded
as a 'model village' housing workers from the
nearby Colman's mustard factory and some of the
front doors are still painted in the firm's distinctive
yellow. The stores are *open Mon-Sat 06.00-20.00
(Sat 07.00) & Sun 08.00-18.00* and *the PO is
technically in Lakenham NR1 3AE.*

Whitlingham Country Park Trowse,
Norwich NR14 8TR (01603 632307; www.
whitlinghamcountrypark.com). A tranquil, get
away from it all location with Whitlingham Great
Broad as its centrepiece. The two-mile wheelchair
accessible path circumnavigates the Broad and
the woodland trails and meadows are well-worth
exploring. There is an abundance of flora, fauna
and fungi and regardless of the time of year there
is always something to see. Cycle-friendly. You can
download a map from the website. Café, toilets and
baby-changing facilities. *Open dawn to dusk.* Free.

● **Thorpe St Andrew**

*Norfolk. PO, stores, chemist, off-licence, takeaways,
fish & chips, butcher, hardware, library, garage.* A
smart residential suburb of Norwich with some
pleasant 18th-C houses in close proximity to the
river, but separated from it by the busy A47 trunk
road. The direct course from Norwich is along
the New Cut which keeps south of the river and
avoids Thorpe altogether. However, if headroom
allows, you can take the original river route, now

a quiet backwater of boathouses and pubs. St
Andrew's church, built in 1866, is approached
through the porch of an earlier building. Its spire,
damaged during the second world war, was
rebuilt in 1956. Thorpe Hall, Grade II* and now
beautifully restored, is an early 17th-C manor
house incorporating parts of a 14th-C building,
and once belonged to the Bishops of Norwich.
The Town House (Hotel) has a superb circular-
domed conservatory, dating from the 1820s. This
building was associated with the Norwich School
of painters whose most celebrated artist was John
Sell Cotman, born in Thorpe in 1782. Many of his
paintings can be seen in the Castle Museum in
Norwich. 'Garden House', a Tudor building, is now
the Rush Cutters pub.

● **Kirby Bedon**

Norfolk. PO box. The church of St Andrew, mainly
19th C but with a genuine Norman south doorway,
faces the ruined round tower of St Mary's.
Together with the Georgian rectory they form a
compact group of attractive buildings just off the
main road.

● **Bramerton**

Norfolk. PO box. A one mile walk up from the
delightful riverside area of Bramerton Woods End.
The church of St Peter dates from the late 13th C
and has a nave built in the Decorated style.

● **Postwick**

Norfolk. PO box. A village surrounded on three
sides by the river and Postwick Marsh with the
railway on the fourth. Parts of All Saints church
date from the late 13th C. It has a Decorated tower
and the piscina (used for washing communion
vessels) is notable.

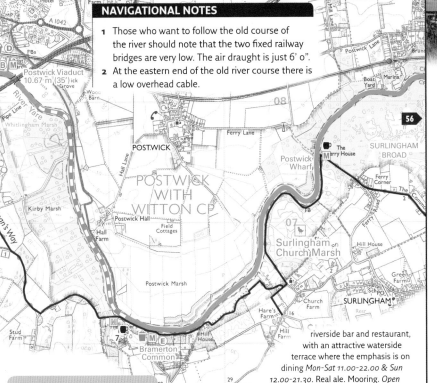

56

NAVIGATIONAL NOTES

1 Those who want to follow the old course of the river should note that the two fixed railway bridges are very low. The air draught is just 6' 0".

2 At the eastern end of the old river course there is a low overhead cable.

BOAT HIRE

Bishy Barney Boats hire electric day boats from Thorpe St Andrew. Contact them at 07810 547779; www.bishybarneyboats.co.uk. Thorpe Ferry Ltd Bungalow Lane, Norwich NR7 0SH also operate a ferry service from Thorpe St Andrew, crossiing the River Yare, and can be contacted at 01603 927412; www.thorpeferry.org.

Pubs and Restaurants

1 The Crown Point Tavern Kirby Road, Trowse Newton, Norwich NR14 8RN (01603 625689; www.crownpointtavern.co.uk). Cosy, two-bar traditional pub on the old Beccles road, dispensing real ale and food *Tue–Sun L and E (not Sun E)*. Garden, dog- and child-friendly. *Open Tue–Sun L and E (not Sun E)*.

2 The Town House 18-22 Yarmouth Road, Thorpe St Andrew, Norwich NR7 0EF (01603 700600; www.stonehouserestaurants.co.uk). Views over the Yare, a large bar and a riverside garden in a carvery pub serving real ale and food *daily 11.30-22.00 (Sun 21.30)*. Wi-Fi. B&B. *Open 11.00-23.00 (Sun 22.30)*.

3 The Rushcutters Arms 46 Yarmouth Road, Thorpe St Andrew, Norwich NR7 0HE (01603 435403; www.chefandbrewer.com). Popular,

riverside bar and restaurant, with an attractive waterside terrace where the emphasis is on dining *Mon–Sat 11.00-22.00 & Sun 12.00-21.30*. Real ale. Mooring. *Open Mon–Sat 11.00-23.00 & Sun 12.00-22.30*. Mooring.

4 The Rivergarden 36 Yarmouth Road, Thorpe St Andrew, Norwich NR7 0EQ (01603 703900; www.therivergardennorwich.com). Compact, riverside pub that enjoys a secluded garden and enticing views over the Yare, dispensing real ale, real cider and food *daily L and E*. Family-friendly. *Open Mon–Thu L and E & Fri–Sun 12.00-23.00 (Sun 22.00)*.

5 The Oak Bar 89 Yarmouth Road, Thorpe St Andrew, Norwich NR7 0HH (01603 434471; www.theoakbarterrace.co.uk). Bar and terrace at the Oaklands Hotel, serving real ale and food *daily L and E*. Family-friendly. Newspapers, sports TV and Wi-Fi. B&B. *Open Mon–Sat 12.00-23.00 (Sun 22.30)*. Mooring.

6 The Merchants of Spice 127 Yarmouth Road, Norwich NR7 0QY (01603 708181; www.merchantsofspice.co.uk). An elegant, relaxing restaurant set in a historic building, serving authentic Indian food using the finest local ingredients, herbs and spices. *Open Tue–Sun 17.00-22.30*. Takeaway service.

7 The Water's Edge Woods End, Bramerton NR14 7ED (01508 538005; www.watersedgewoodsend.co.uk). 17th-C riverside inn offering modern, à la carte and bar menus – *Mon–Sat L and E & Sun 12.00-19.00* – in an oak-beamed dining room, with views overlooking the River Yare. Real ale. Garden, family-friendly. Wi-Fi. *Open daily 11.00-01.00 (Sun 21.00)*. Mooring.

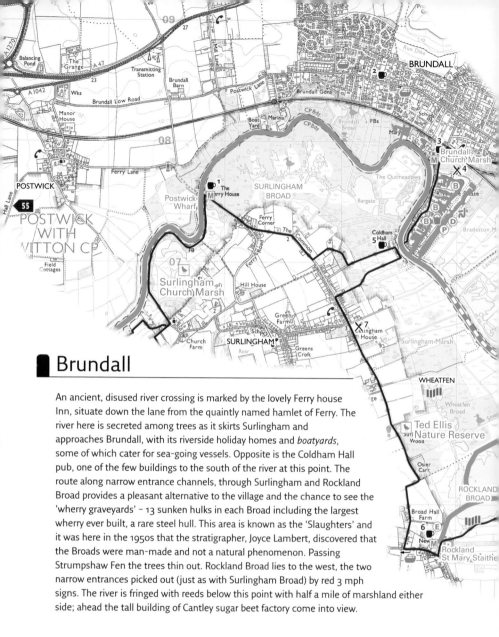

Brundall

An ancient, disused river crossing is marked by the lovely Ferry house Inn, situate down the lane from the quaintly named hamlet of Ferry. The river here is secreted among trees as it skirts Surlingham and approaches Brundall, with its riverside holiday homes and *boatyards*, some of which cater for sea-going vessels. Opposite is the Coldham Hall pub, one of the few buildings to the south of the river at this point. The route along narrow entrance channels, through Surlingham and Rockland Broad provides a pleasant alternative to the village and the chance to see the 'wherry graveyards' – 13 sunken hulks in each Broad including the largest wherry ever built, a rare steel hull. This area is known as the 'Slaughters' and it was here in the 1950s that the stratigrapher, Joyce Lambert, discovered that the Broads were man-made and not a natural phenomenon. Passing Strumpshaw Fen the trees thin out. Rockland Broad lies to the west, the two narrow entrances picked out (just as with Surlingham Broad) by red 3 mph signs. The river is fringed with reeds below this point with half a mile of marshland either side; ahead the tall building of Cantley sugar beet factory come into view.

● **Surlingham**
Norfolk. PO box, farm shop. A sprawling village to the south of Surlingham Broad from where you can access the little RSPB Surlingham Church Marsh Nature reserve. The church is situated to the east of the village. Dedicated to St Mary, it has a round Norman tower topped with a 14th-C octagonal belfry. A short distance to the north east are the ruins of St Saviours thought to have been built in 12thC.

● **Brundall**
Norfolk. Stores, off-licence, fish & chips, takeaway, hardware, station. A village of commuters and Broadland holiday makers, distinguished for its abundance of charming cottages and riverside villas. A vast marina south of the station makes a base for many boat hire companies; on summer weekends the water is thick with craft. The tiny 13th-C church of St Lawrence stands in the midst of fields to the east, aloof from such worldly

doings. It has the only lead font in Norfolk and some nice 16th-C stained glass.

● Rockland St Mary

Norfolk. Stores, off-licence. A linear village to the west of Rockland Broad. The church of St Mary dates from the 14th C, with much rebuilding. To the north is Wheatfen Broad, maintained by the Ted Ellis Trust (www.wheatfen.org/explore/the-reserve) as a nature reserve. Ted Ellis (1909-1986) was a writer and broadcaster who was one of the most-well known and respected naturalists in East Anglia and beyond.

● Strumpshaw

Norfolk. PO box. A tiny village on the slopes of Strumpshaw Hill. It is worth visiting the church of St Peter to have a look at the colourful 15th-C screen. Every Boxing day morning the 'poor' of the village gather in the church porch, each to receive a share from four bushels of wheat. This Strumpshaw tradition, unbroken for more than 250 years, comes from the last will and testament of a local farmer – William Black – who decreed that the distribution should be made from his estate forever.

Strumpshaw Fen Low Road, Strumpshaw, Norwich NR13 4HS (01603 715191; www.rspb.org.uk/reserves-and-events/reserves-a-z/strumpshaw-fen). A complete range of Broadland habitats and wildlife with five miles of mown footpaths, Strumpshaw Fen offers the chance to walk around reedbeds, woodlands and orchid-rich meadows where the visitor is likely to come upon marsh harriers, bitterns, bearded tits and kingfishers. Visitor Centre, café, picnic area, nature trails, guided walks, viewing points and binocular hire. Charge for non-RSPB members.

Strumpshaw Steam Museum Old Hall, Strumpshaw NR13 4HR (01603 714535; www.strumpshawsteammuseum.co.uk). All manner of steam engines (26 in all) including a working 100-ton beam engine, a narrow gauge railway, a showman's road engine and mechanical fairground organs dating from the 1930s. Collection of rare breeds. Engines in steam last Sun of month. Café, shop and memorabilia. Well-behaved dogs welcome. *Open Apr-Sep, Sun & B Hols 10.30-15.30.* Charge.

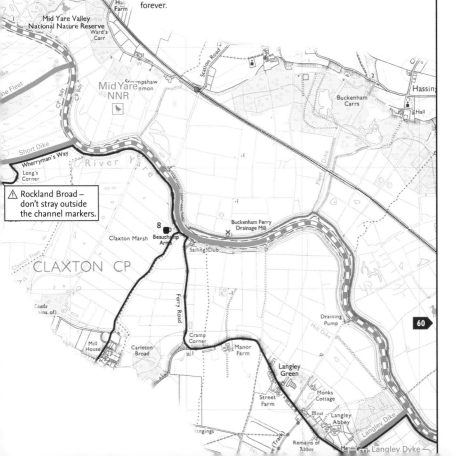

1 The Ferry House 1 Ferry Road, Surlingham NR14 7AR (01508 538659; www.surlinghamferry. co.uk). Traditional, and very characterful riverside country pub, opened in 1725, serving real ale and real cider together with a selection of excellent homemade food *daily 09.00-21.00*. Breakfast from *09.00 – on request*. Garden, dog- and child-friendly. Quiz *Fri* and *regular* live music. Real fires, newspapers, traditional pub games and Wi-fi. *Open 09.00-23.00*. Mooring.

2 The Ram Inn 108 The Street, Brundall NR13 5LP (01603 712569). Plucked from the grasp of Tesco a decade ago, this friendly, two-bar local now serves real ale and food *Tue-Sun L and E (not Sun E)*. Huge garden with children's play area. Live music *Sun*. Traditional pub games and Wi-fi. *Open 12.00-23.00 (Fri-Sat 23.30)*.

3 The Yare at Brundall Riverside Estate, Brundall NR13 5PL (01603 713786; www.facebook. com/pages/The-Yare-pub/172947919390949). Close to the railway station, sandwiched in amongst the boatyards, this is a popular pub *in summer* serving real ale and food *Mon-Thu E & Fri-Sun L and E*. Family-friendly, garden. Traditional pub games and real fires. *Open 11.00-23.00 (closed Mon-Thu L out of season)*.

4 East Hills Café Bistro Brundall Bay Marina, Riverside Estate, Brundall NR13 5PN (01630 951850; www.facebook.com/ easthillscafebistro). Close to the railway station but almost lost in a jumble of boatyards, this cafe/bistro serves local seafood alongside classic cafe dishes. Heated terrace. Breakfast available *09.30-12.00. Open Wed-Sat 09.30-23.00 (Wed 22.00) & Sun 09.30-18.00*.

5 Coldham Hall Tavern Coldham Hall, Surlingham NR14 7AN (01508 538366; www. coldhamhalltavern.com). Real ales and meals sourced from local ingredients are the staple of this picturesque, riverside pub with superb views along the Yare. Food is available *Mon-Sat L and E & Sun 12.00-18.00 (16.00 out of season). Regular* live music. Garden, dog- and child-friendly. Traditional pub games, real fires and Wi-fi. *Open 12.00-23.00 (Sun 21.00)*. Moorings

6 The New Inn 12 New Inn Hill, Rockland St Mary NR14 7HP (01508 538211; www.facebook. com/NewInnRSM). A village local offering a good selection of real ales and homemade food *L and E*. Patio, dog- and child-friendly. *Regular* live music. Traditional pub games, real fires and Wi-fi. *Open Mon-Sat 11.00-23.00 (Fri-Sat 01.00) & Sun 12.00-00.00*.

7 Teles Patisserie Mill Road, Surlingham NR14 7GD (01508 538892; www.telespatisserie.co.uk). Beside the Yare Valley Farm Shop. For walkers and cyclists, it can also be approached via The Covey at NR14 7AL. Select from the appetising breakfast and lunch menus or pick from a selection of delicious pastries, fresh bread and afternoon teas. Also fresh coffee and cold drinks which you can enjoy both inside or in the picturesque courtyard. *Open Tue-Sun 10.00-16.00*. Wi-fi.

8 The Beauchamp Arms Ferry Road, Langley NR14 6DH (01508 480247; www.beauchamparms. uk). Large, multi-roomed pub in a remote location, serving real ale and food *L and E*. Riverside garden. Traditional pub games and real fires. Camping. Mooring. *Open 12.00-23.00 (Sun 22.30)*.

Loddon

A generous meandering course is taken across the marshes by the wide reed-fringed river. Towers of disused windpumps are passed at frequent intervals and more are seen in the distance. Langley Dike provides an interesting diversion before passing Cantley where the sugar beet factory (originally built in 1912) brings a flavour of the industrial waterways to the Broads, reminding us that the whole of this network was once used as a commercial transport system, long before the coming of the railways and roads. The factory has continued to expand over the years and is now one of only four remaining in the UK where once there were 17. Between them, they now process 1.3 million tonnes of sugar beet sourced from 750 British growers. Joining the main river by the Hardley Cross – marking the boundary of the jurisdiction of the City of Norwich and erected in 1676 – is the lovely River Chet; time should be found to visit Loddon and Chedgrave. Heading up this three-mile tributary the navigator cannot fail to notice the limited width and elevated position – rather like a canal on a low embankment. Twisting and turning it passes Hardley Flood, separated from it in one place only by a wooden footbridge carrying the path. Keep a look out for stacks of cut reeds, for use as thatch, lying at the water's edge. A succession of boatyards signal the virtual limit of navigation and the staithe is soon reached. A clapboarded mill finally closes the river while on the main river the chain ferry, the last on the Broads, indicates the approach to Reedham.

NAVIGATIONAL NOTES

1 Hardley Dike is very narrow and it is difficult to turn. There are no facilities here.
2 Reedham Chain Ferry – keep well clear when it is crossing and remember that the chains stretch right across the river from bank to bank.

● **Cantley**
Norfolk. PO box, station. A market town during the 13th C, Cantley is now a village dominated by the vast sugar-beet factory. Smoke billows from the chimneys during the autumn and winter months that the crop is being processed and the sugar extracted. Sugar-beet is a major part of the local farming economy and one of the few root crops grown amongst the cereal and rape which predominates here. The church of St Margaret dates mainly from 14th C, incorporating earlier Norman work.

● **Langley Green**
Norfolk. PO box. Scattered village approached via Langley Dike. Just to the west are the few flint remains, some incorporated into farm buildings, of Langley Abbey founded by Premonstratensian Canons in 1195. It is built on a gravel outcrop surrounded by peat. The church and Langley Park are over a mile to the south west.

● **Hardley Street**
Norfolk. Just a little more than a quarter of a mile from Hardley Staithe is the church of St Margaret's. It has a round Norman tower and a 15th-C wall painting of St Christopher. There are ample opportunities for walking in this area, with good footpaths and quiet lanes – an excellent three-mile ramble, starting at the church, would pass Hardley Hall, a 16th-C house, progress east to the River Chet and then south along the river bank by Hardley Flood (a 120-acre SSSI rich in birdlife) to finish at the White Horse pub in Chedgrave. Less energetic crew members can bring the boat round!

● **Loddon (and Chedgrave)**
Norfolk. PO, stores, chemist, fish & chips, takeaways, off-licence, laundrette, library. Loddon, to the south of the Chet, has a main street lined with attractive, mainly Georgian houses, with the market square and church to the east. Holy Trinity – late 15th C and much-restored Perpendicular – stands in a vast graveyard. Light floods in through the many windows, illuminating the unusual screen, decorated with scenes from the Life of Christ and Martyrdom of Sir William of Norwich, who is shown with blood gushing from his side. It is thought by some that the original church on this site was founded by St Felix in 630. The oak alms box is a relic thought to have come from this building. Anglo-Saxon, it is carved from a solid block of wood. There are some excellent brasses and monuments – that to Lady Williamson, patron of several London churches, is of particular note. A painting the south aisle depicts Sir James Hobart and his wife against a background of Loddon church and, interestingly, a fortified bridge at St Olaves. The Hobart family lived at Hales Hall and were responsible for the building

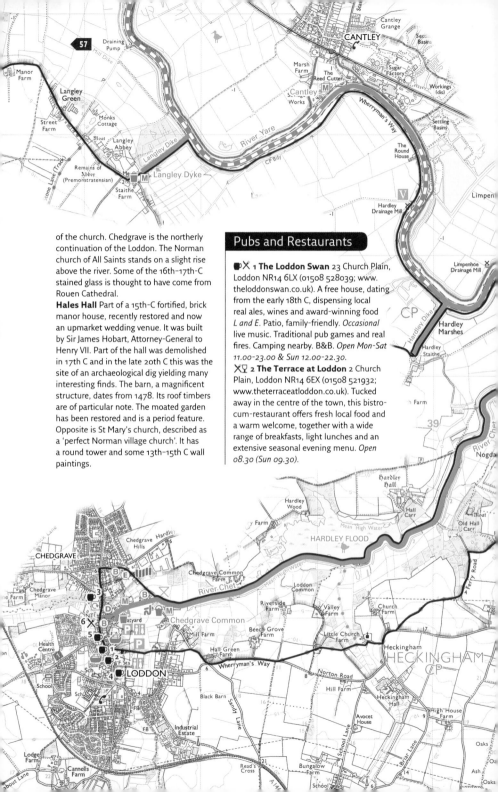

of the church. Chedgrave is the northerly continuation of the Loddon. The Norman church of All Saints stands on a slight rise above the river. Some of the 16th–17th-C stained glass is thought to have come from Rouen Cathedral.

Hales Hall Part of a 15th-C fortified, brick manor house, recently restored and now an upmarket wedding venue. It was built by Sir James Hobart, Attorney-General to Henry VII. Part of the hall was demolished in 17th C and in the late 20th C this was the site of an archaeological dig yielding many interesting finds. The barn, a magnificent structure, dates from 1478. Its roof timbers are of particular note. The moated garden has been restored and is a period feature. Opposite is St Mary's church, described as a 'perfect Norman village church'. It has a round tower and some 13th–15th C wall paintings.

Pubs and Restaurants

1 The Loddon Swan 23 Church Plain, Loddon NR14 6LX (01508 528039; www.theloddonswan.co.uk). A free house, dating from the early 18th C, dispensing local real ales, wines and award-winning food *L and E*. Patio, family-friendly. *Occasional* live music. Traditional pub games and real fires. Camping nearby. B&B. *Open Mon-Sat 11.00-23.00 & Sun 12.00-22.30.*

2 The Terrace at Loddon 2 Church Plain, Loddon NR14 6EX (01508 521932; www.theterraceatloddon.co.uk). Tucked away in the centre of the town, this bistro-cum-restaurant offers fresh local food and a warm welcome, together with a wide range of breakfasts, light lunches and an extensive seasonal evening menu. *Open 08.30 (Sun 09.30).*

3 The White Horse 5 Norwich Road, Chedgrave NR14 6ND (01508 520250; www.whitehorsechedgrave.co.uk). Within easy reach of the moorings at Loddon, this welcoming hostelry serves real ale and food *Mon-Sat L and E & Sun 12.00-19.30*. Garden, dog- and family-friendly. Traditional pub games, real fires and Wi-Fi. Camping nearby. *Open 12.00-00.00 (Sun 22.00)*.

4 The Angel 15 High Street, Loddon NR14 6ET (01508 520699). Well-kept, town-centre pub with three small cosy bars. Real ale and bar snacks available *all day*. Meals served *L and E*. Traditional pub games. *Open daily 12.00-23.00*.

5 The Kings Head 16 Bridge Street, Loddon NR14 6EZ (01508 520330; www.facebook.com/loddonkingshead). Bar, restaurant and real ales in a charming old setting. Excellent home-cooked food served *L and E*. Sports TV. *Open 11.00-23.00 (Sun 22.30)*.

6 Rosy Lee's 37A Bridge Street, Loddon NR14 6NA (01508 520204; www.facebook.com/rosyleesloddon). A small, friendly cafe serving a wide range of inexpensive, locally sourced food and drink. Daily specials and delicious high teas. *Open Wed-Mon 08.00-17.00 (Sun 09.00)*.

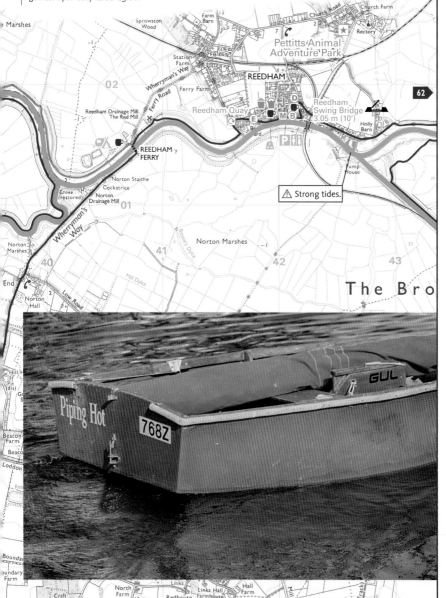

Reedham

Below Reedham Railway Swing Bridge, Haddiscoe New Cut provides a (dull) shortcut to Oulton Broad and the River Waveney, while the Yare meanders across a vast expanse of marsh to Berney Arms. To the north is Breydon Water, to the south is the Waveney which makes its lonely course across the marshes to St Olaves. Reedham Ferry is the only traditional chain ferry left on the Broads and is adjacent to the popular Reedham Ferry Inn and *campsite*.

● **Reedham**
Norfolk. PO, stores, fish & chips, off-licence, station.
It was here that a 'King's Falconer' murdered Lothbroc the Dane; the bad feeling that this generated caused 20,000 Danes to take Norfolk by force, thus ending the Saxon dynasty. Today, as a result of a minor blossoming of industry up to 1900, the village is mainly Victorian and the riverside – as you'd expect – is very busy *during the summer*. To the west is the chain ferry, the last on the Broads and the only road crossing of the Yare between Yarmouth and Norwich, while to the east is an unusual railway swing bridge, drawn aside for the tall-masted sailing yachts that criss-cross the river. The church of St John Baptist stands on higher ground to the north east. In Roman times Reedham was a coastal location and remnants of the Roman lighthouse can still be found in the church. The fish and chip shop is *open Thu-Sat, L and E*.
Reedham also contains **Pettitts Animal Park** half a mile from the waterfront and adjacent to it the Humpty Dumpty Brewery (01493 701818; www. humptydumptybrewery.co.uk) *open Easter-Oct daily 12.00-17.00* selling a range of craft beers, gins and gifts.
RSPB Berney Marshes Berney Marshes, Burgh Castle NR31 9PZ (01493 700645; www.rspb.org.uk/reserves-and-events/reserves-a-z/berney-marshes-breydon-water). The RSPB maintain over 1300 acres of improved wet grassland for up to 85,000 wintering wildfowl and waders, notable species being golden plover, lapwing, pink-footed goose, redshank and wigeon. They manage ditches for the benefit of aquatic invertebrates and other wildlife and maintain almost a thousand acres of intertidal mud and saltmarsh for the wintering wildfowl.

● **Burgh Castle**
Norfolk. PO box, shop, chemist, fish & chips, takeaway, station (distant at Berney Arms).
The village lies back from the river, behind the marina and holiday village. A short walk to the north, overlooking the Waveney, are the substantial remains of the 3rd-C Roman fort of Garianonum, encompassing an area of six acres and affording good views towards Berney Arms, the marshes to the west and Breydon Water to the north. A short way from the fort is the church of St Peter and St Paul, which has a Norman round tower and bench ends decorated with poppy heads.
Berney Arms Mill NR30 1SB (01493 700645; www.english-heritage.org.uk/visit/places/berney-arms-windmill/directions). One of Norfolk's best-preserved and largest extant marsh mills, built in 1912 to grind a constituent of cement and in use until 1948. Subsequently it was re-purposed for pumping water to drain surrounding marshland. Located in a great area for birdwatching with fine views across the marshes. *Access to mill by pre-booked tours, telephone to confirm availability*. Charge.

⚠ Keep clear of banks – submerged piling along the New Cut.

NAVIGATIONAL NOTES

1   Do not cut the corner at Berney Arms – keep to the marked channel.
2   When tying up at Reedham, always moor facing into the tide which is especially strong here.

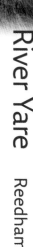

Polkey's and Cadge's Mills NR13 3UB (01362 869394; www.norfolk.gov.uk/out-and-about-in-norfolk/windmills). Two drainage mills out of an original cluster of three, situated close to Seven Mile House. Polkey's Mill was built sometime prior to 1880 and is now fully restored. Now brick but the old cap is retained. The mill drove a scoop-wheel (a paddle wheel in a brick channel) which lifted the water from the marshes, through a hinged gate, into the river. Cadge's Mill is minus cap and sails. It was also built around 1880 and last worked in 1941. The site also includes Reedham Marsh Steam Engine House and the restored (and working) Ruston diesel pumping engines. Telephone *for opening times* when the machinery is usually in operation.

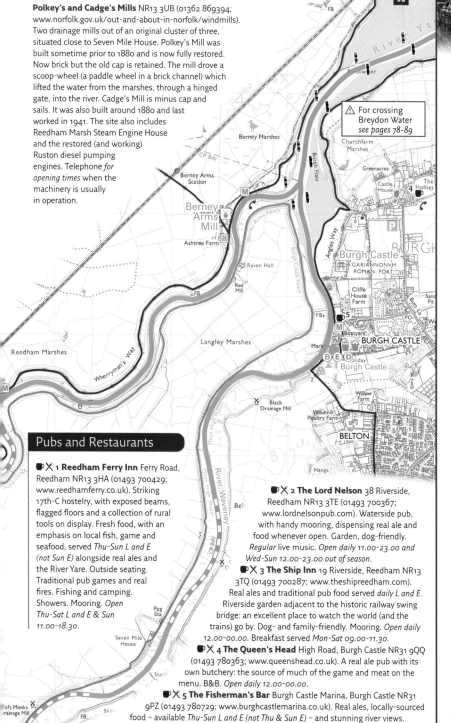

Pubs and Restaurants

◗✕ **1 Reedham Ferry Inn** Ferry Road, Reedham NR13 3HA (01493 700429; www.reedhamferry.co.uk). Striking 17th-C hostelry, with exposed beams, flagged floors and a collection of rural tools on display. Fresh food, with an emphasis on local fish, game and seafood, served *Thu-Sun L and E (not Sun E)* alongside real ales and the River Yare. Outside seating. Traditional pub games and real fires. Fishing and camping. Showers. Mooring. *Open Thu-Sat L and E & Sun 11.00-18.30.*

◗✕ **2 The Lord Nelson** 38 Riverside, Reedham NR13 3TE (01493 700367; www.lordnelsonpub.com). Waterside pub, with handy mooring, dispensing real ale and food whenever open. Garden, dog-friendly. *Regular* live music. *Open daily 11.00-23.00 and Wed-Sun 12.00-23.00 out of season.*

◗✕ **3 The Ship Inn** 19 Riverside, Reedham NR13 3TQ (01493 700287; www.theshipreedham.com). Real ales and traditional pub food served *daily L and E*. Riverside garden adjacent to the historic railway swing bridge: an excellent place to watch the world (and the trains) go by. Dog- and family-friendly. Mooring. *Open daily 12.00-00.00.* Breakfast served *Mon-Sat 09.00-11.30.*

◗✕ **4 The Queen's Head** High Road, Burgh Castle NR31 9QQ (01493 780363; www.queenshead.co.uk). A real ale pub with its own butchery: the source of much of the game and meat on the menu. B&B. *Open daily 12.00-00.00.*

◗✕ **5 The Fisherman's Bar** Burgh Castle Marina, Burgh Castle NR31 9PZ (01493 780729; www.burghcastlemarina.co.uk). Real ales, locally-sourced food – available *Thu-Sun L and E (not Thu & Sun E)* – and stunning river views. Children and well-behaved dogs welcome. Mooring. *Open daily 12.00-23.00.*

63

THE RIVER WAVENEY

The Broads Authority publish guidance to the River Waveney at www.broads-authority.gov.uk/boating/navigating-the-broads/water-depths/river-waveney which includes further helpful tips and can be read in conjunction with this guide. These are particularly useful for water depth, speed limits and channel details which can alter regularly due to bank works and tidal movement.

The source of the Waveney is to be found five miles west of Diss, less than half a mile from the point where the River Little Ouse rises to flow west from the watershed into the Fenlands. In 1670 an Act of Parliament was passed giving authority to improve the navigation from Beccles to Bungay by building locks at Gedleston, Ellingham and Wainford on what was a private navigation outside the jurisdiction of the Yarmouth Commissioners. After changing ownership several times, this section was finally abandoned in 1934.

During the early part of 19th C the merchants of Beccles felt aggrieved, as did their counterparts in Norwich, that all goods had to be transhipped at Yarmouth and were equally delighted when, in 1831, the new route through Oulton Dike, Oulton Broad and Lake Lothing to the sea at Lowestoft was opened. However, by around 1850, due to silting, boats were once again trading via Yarmouth. Today only pleasure craft use the river and have to turn below the site of Gedleston Lock. Built in 1670, it is the current limit of navigation and over an eight year period has been the subject of restoration by the IWA Waterways recovery Group, supported by the River Waveney Trust and completed in 2021. From its source to the junction into Haddiscoe New Cut, the river constitutes the boundary between Norfolk and Suffolk.

Beccles

The character of the River Waveney is soon established as it meanders across the flood plain, the villages keeping their distance along the higher ground. Gedleston, however, can be reached via Gedleston Dyke. Beccles lies to the east behind an attractive but brief river frontage. Once through the low bridge the river again enters marshland, with woodland below the Stanley Hills bringing a welcome change.

NAVIGATIONAL NOTES

1 The abandoned Gedleston Lock, beside the Locks Inn, is the limit of navigation.
2 At Beccles Bridge there is only 6' 6" air draught at mean high water spring tides.

● **Bungay**
Suffolk. PO, stores, chemist, off-licence, fish & chips, takeaways, delicatessen, butcher, greengrocer, hardware, off-licence, library. A handsome market town with over a thousand years of history – indeed the Mayor of Bungay is still known as the Town Reeve: a Saxon term. Of interest are: the castle ruins; Holy Trinity Church, which has an 11th-C round tower, one of the oldest in the country; and the Butter Cross. Built in 1689, this octagonal domed shelter from which butter and other produce was sold, once contained both a dungeon and a cage for prisoners. The town is still accessible by canoe.

Bungay Castle 6 Cross Street, Bungay NR35 1AU (01986 892721; www.bungay-suffolk.co.uk/attractions-bungay-castle-castle-hills). The Bigods were a powerful Norman family who assisted King William with the Conquest of England in 1066. As a reward for their support, he granted them manors and lands throughout East Anglia, including Bungay and Framlingham. Both the Bigod family and the castle subsequently enjoyed a colourful history as the website attests. When Dr Leonard Cane became the Town Reeve of Bungay in 1934 he organised a programme of excavation and repair, rebuilding parts of the decayed walls, and revealing many features which had been hidden during the last centuries. In 1987 the castle was presented to the town by the Duke of Norfolk with an endowment towards its preservation. It is now owned and administered by the Castle Trust. Access to the castle is through the courtyard and cafe 'Bigod's Kitchen' which is adjacent to the castle. There is an interpretive model of the castle on display in the cafe courtyard. *Open 24 hours.* Donations.

Bungay Museum Council Office, Broad Street, Bungay NR35 1EE (01986 893155). Local history museum currently housed on the first floor of the Waveney District Council offices.

Norfolk and Suffolk Aviation Museum Bungay The Street, Flixton, Bungay NR35 1NZ (01985 896644; www.aviationmuseum.net). The joint themes of this collection are the occupation of the airfield by the 446th Bomber Group USAAF (briefly followed by the Fleet Air Arm and then the RAF) and aviation in the east of England. These broad headings have permitted a very varied collection of aircraft and artefacts to be gathered and displayed and virtually everything has been donated by visitors. The collection continues to grow! NAAFI and shop. *Open Wed & Sat-Sun 10.00-16.00.*

● **Gedleston**
Norfolk. PO box, farm shop. A small village at the limit of navigation on the Waveney, notable for having two fine pubs one of which, situated by the disused lock, has recently been the subject of a successful community buy out. The lock once marked the start of an extended navigation to Bungay. The church of St Michael has a round tower but little other original work. There are some fine headstones in the churchyard. There is an excellent, well-stocked farm shop a little to the west of the village, selling a range of seasonal farm produce, together with fresh bread and milk – Geldeston Road, Bungay NR35 2ER (01508 518273).

● **Barsham**
Suffolk. Farm shop. Follow the footpath south to Locks Lane and turn left where it meets the main road. In half a mile you will find Holy Trinity church, Barsham. Its round tower is topped with a spike but the real delight is the whole exterior of the east wall, an amazing flint lattice (undated but pre-17th C) spreading across the face which incorporates a stained glass east window by Kempe. Inside there are fine examples of more recent work: the stuccoed chancel roof (1906) and the gaily decorated rood canopy.

● **Gillingham**
Norfolk. PO box. A modern estate village. Separate and to the north, is the Norman church of St Mary. The nave was rebuilt in 1859 in the Norman style. Only the tower remains of All Saints, its close neighbour. The rest of the building collapsed in 1748. Both are Grade I listed and are accompanied by a later ecclesiastical sibling in the form of the pretty, Grade II Roman Catholic Chapel of Ease daring from 1898 and modelled on Santissima Trinità dei Monti: a famous church in Rome. Brick-

built and fronted by two symmetrical bell towers, it was designed by a Frederick Banham, a Beccles architect, and commissioned by John Kenyon of Gillingham Hall.

● **Beccles**
Suffolk. PO, stores, chemist, takeaways, fish & chips, off-licence, hardware, library, garage, station. A solidly Georgian town, rebuilt in red brick after four great fires in 16th C and 17th C. With lock-free access to the sea it was once a great port, with Norfolk wherries and bluff-bowed 'billyboy' ketches from the north east filling the quays. Today the waterfront has a more genteel air, with long gardens running down to private moorings, each with its smart cruiser. Since the printer William Clowes moved out of the town to nearby Ellough, in 2004, there has been little industry and even that is remarkable inconspicuous. From the river, the tower of St Michael's is dominant. Separate from the body of the church, it is 97ft tall, square and solid. Sold for £1 in 1972 to the local council, who had to assume ownership before starting restoration, the view from the top is well worth the climb. The church has a very grand south porch, two storeys tall with much detailed decoration. However, the interior, destroyed by fire in 1586, is of little architectural interest. It was here, on 11th May 1749, Rev Edmund Nelson and Catherine Suckling were married; their son was Horatio Nelson the British naval hero.
Beccles Lido Puddingmoor, Beccles NR34 9PL

(01502 713297; www.beccleslido.com). Riverside, outdoor pool heated *during the summer* to 28 deg C. Children's adventure play and picnic area. Café. *Open daily 07.00-22.00.* Mooring. Charge. The Big Dog Ferry (www.facebook.com/bigdogferrybeccles) operates from here. See Boat Trips.
Beccles & District Museum Leman House, Ballygate, Beccles NR34 9ND (01502 715722; www.becclesmuseum.org.uk). Housed in a magnificent 16th-C building, constructed in the early 1500s and restored and modernised in the 1760s. This local and natural history museum is manned entirely by unpaid volunteers. Displays range from a few Iron Age and Roman items to a large number of Victorian artefacts, including a scale model of 1854 Beccles. Large historical photographic collection of local people and places and a growing historical database of Beccles clockmakers. *Open Apr-Oct, Tue-Sun & B Hol Mon 13.45-16.30.* Free. Donations.
Broads Information Centre The Library, Blyburgate, Beccles NR34 9TB (01502 523442). *Open Mon-Sat 09.30-17.00 (Fri 19.30).*
There is a handy cycle shop on the north eastern edge of the town: **Pedalz Bicycle Shop** Common Lane North, Beccles NR34 9BL (011502 718724; https://www.facebook.com/pedalz.co.uk). *Open Wed-Sat 09.30-17.30 (Sat 16.30) & Sun 10.00-15.00.*

Pubs and Restaurants

🍺 1 **The Green Dragon** 29 Broad Street, Bungay NR35 1EE (01986 892581; www.greendragonbungay.co.uk). Home to the Green Dragon Brewery, serving an excellent selection of their real ales and *occasional* food. Garden, dog- and child-friendly. Traditional pub games and Wi-Fi. *Occasional* live music. Camping nearby. *Open Mon-Fri 11.00-00.00 & Sat-Sun 12.00-00.00 (Sun 21.00).*

🍺✕ 2 **The Olive Tree** 28 Old Yarmouth Road, Ellingham, Kirby Row, Bungay NR35 2PN (01508 518147; www.olive-tree-restaurant.co.uk).

Authentic Mediterranean menu served *L and E* in a delightful ambiance in this highly thought of, village bar-cum-restaurant. No real ale however. *Open daily 12.00-23.00 (Sun 22.30). Telephone to confirm food serving times before travelling.*

🍺✕ 3 **The Artichoke** 162 Yarmouth Road, Broome, Bungay NR35 2NZ (01986 893325; www.facebook.com/theArtichokeatBroome). Gravity-fed beers from local breweries dominate this excellent selection of real ales, while appetising home-cooked food is available *Tue-Sun L and E (not Sun E).* Also real cider. Garden, dogs and children welcome. Real fires and Wi-Fi. Camping nearby. *Open Tue-Thu L and E & Fri-Sun 12.00-23.00.*

🍺 4 **The Fleece Inn**
8-10 St Mary's

△ CAUTION – overhead cables.

WALKING AND CYCLING
The footpath, which starts at Gedleston Dyke, makes a pleasant walk into Beccles.

Street, Bungay NR35 1AX (01986 897079; www.thefleeceinnbungay.co.uk). Real ale is dispensed in this 17th-C, low-ceiled hostelry with exposed beams, together with food *Mon-Sat L and E & Sun 12.00-20.00*. Courtyard seating, dog- and child-friendly. Real fires and Wi-Fi. *Open Mon-Sat 11.00-22.00 (Fri-Sat 23.00) & Sun 12.00-21.00*.

5 The Locks Inn Lock's Lane, Gedleston NR34 0HS (01508 830033;www.thelocksinn.com). This riverside pub, parts still lit by candles, is a wee gem and we have the local community to thank for its continued existence. Real ales, pop up catering (*Fri night* is curry night) and, once the kitchens are refurbished, the prospect of hearty, home-cooked fayre. Dog- and family-friendly, garden. *Regular* live music nights. Traditional pub games and real fires. Camping and mooring. *Open Sun-Wed 11.00-20.00 & Thu-Sat 11.00-22.00. (E only in winter)*.

6 The Wherry Inn 7 The Street, Gedleston NR34 0LB (01508 518371; www.wherryinn.co.uk). Delightfully restored village pub serving real ales with secret courtyards and a garden. Excellent homemade pub food available *Mon-Sat L and E* and *Sun 12.00-18.00*. Garden, dog and child-friendly. Traditional pub games, real fires and Wi-Fi. Pub *open daily 12.00-23.00*. Tearoom attached *open Fri-Sun 11.00-16.00* Mooring

7 The Swan Motel Loddon Road, Gillingham, Beccles NR34 0LD (01502 470047; www.gillinghamswan.co.uk). The original Swan was built in 1789, now long gone and replaced by a modern building, serving real ale and plentiful helpings of food *L and E*. Garden, dog- and family-friendly. Traditional pub games and Wi-Fi. B&B. *Open daily 11.00-23.00 (Sun 22.30)*.

8 The Bear & Bells 11 Old Market, Beccles NR34 9AP (01502 712291; www.bearandbells.co.uk). Handy for the bus station,

this 19th-C Victorian hostelry serves real ale and food *Tue-Sun L and E (not Sun E)*. Rear terrace, dog- and child-friendly. Wi-Fi. *Open Tue-Fri L and E & Sat-Sun 10.00-22.00 (Sun 16.00)*.

9 The Swan House Restaurant 34 New Market, Beccles NR34 9HE (01502 713474; www.swan-house.com). Bar and restaurant in a Grade II listed building serving mezze-style dishes and cold platters. No real ale. Patio area. B&B. *Open daily 12.00-19.30*.

10 The Caxton Arms 1 Ravensmere, Beccles NR34 9DY (01502 470002). A locals' street corner pub with juke box and a fruit machine, serving real ale, which often includes a dark beer. Dog-friendly. Traditional pub games and Wi-Fi. *Open Mon-Sat 11.00-23.00 & Sun 12.00-22.30*.

11 The Butchers Arms 51 London Road, Beccles NR34 9YT (01502 712243; www.mypub.org.uk). Open-plan pub on the edge of the town, offering a range of events and music nights, dispensing a good selection of real ales, often from East Anglian breweries, together with real cider. Garden, dog-friendly. Regular live music. Traditional pub games, real fires and sports TV. *Open Mon-Thu 16.00-00.00 & Fri-Sun 12.00-00.30 (Sun 00.00)*.

12 The Shadingfield Fox London Road, Shadingfield, Beccles NR34 8DD (01502 575100; www.shadingfieldfox.com). Dating from 16th C, this comfortable country pub serves a good selection of real ales and food *Wed-Sat L and E & Sun 12.00-18.00*. Garden, dog-friendly. *Sun* live music. Wi-Fi, book and real ale clubs. *Open Mon-Tue 16.00-close & Wed-Sun 12.00-close*.

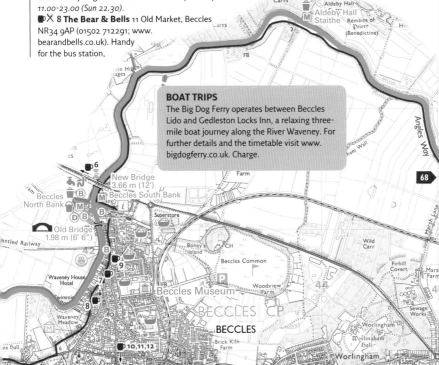

BOAT TRIPS
The Big Dog Ferry operates between Beccles Lido and Gedleston Locks Inn, a relaxing three-mile boat journey along the River Waveney. For further details and the timetable visit www.bigdogferry.co.uk. Charge.

New Bridge 3.66 m (12')

Old Bridge 1.98 m (6' 6")

Beccles Museum

BECCLES

Burgh St Peter

A very remote but attractive stretch of river, with a wide expanse of marshland either side and not a road in sight until the Waveney Inn is reached. The Waveney forms the county boundary between Norfolk and Suffolk and low lying land beside the river forms a series of levels in the parish of Burgh St Peter, the largest of which is Burgh Marshes to the north east of the village. There were once two mills on this section of the river, one pumped water from the drainage ditches and the other ground corn. Of the latter there is now no sign (although reference was made to its ruinous state in the 1920s) while the stump of the former now forms the basis of a private dwelling.

● **Aldeby**

Norfolk. PO. A tiny village with some modern housing. The church of St Mary is a Norman building with evidence of restoration. It has a nicely decorated 14th-C porch. By Aldeby Hall are the remains of a Benedictine Priory and an ancient burial ground. The Mobile Post Office Common Road, 1 Laburnum Cottage, Aldeby NR34 0BL (01502 677750) is *open Mon 08.45-11.15 & Thu 08.45-12.15.*

● **Burgh St Peter**

Norfolk. Stores, PO box. A scattered village which adjoins Wheatacre where the Church of All saints is situated.

The sturdy brick and flint Perpendicular tower has been built with a bold chequerboard pattern beneath a battlemented top. The interior of the nave suggests 14th C origins and the font and font cover are both notable. The actual village church of Burgh St Peter lies one and a half miles to the east, on a slight prominence between the River Waveney and Burgh Marshes. The charming 13th-C thatched nave is unfortunately dominated by a grotesque folly of a tower – four brick boxes

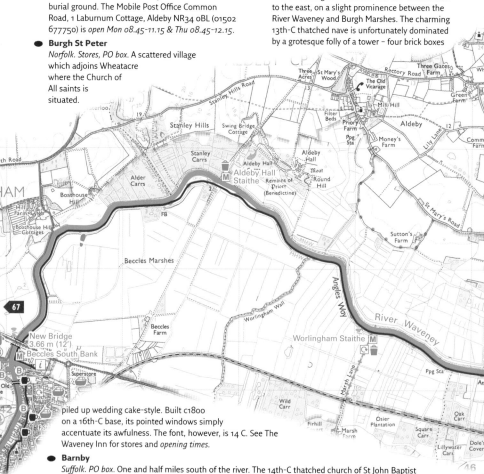

piled up wedding cake-style. Built c1800 on a 16th-C base, its pointed windows simply accentuate its awfulness. The font, however, is 14 C. See The Waveney Inn for stores and *opening times.*

● **Barnby**

Suffolk. PO box. One and half miles south of the river. The 14th-C thatched church of St John Baptist has a 13th-C font and Banner Staff Locker with a traceried door – possibly a unique feature. **Sam's Bicycles** 11 Fir Close, Barnby, Beccles NR34 7QE (01502 476320/07812 640184; www.samsbicycles. co.uk). Helpful, friendly and flexible service *open Mon-Fri 09.00-18.00 & Sat 14.00-17.00.*

Pubs and Restaurants (pages xx-xx)

🍴✕ **1 The Three Horseshoes** Old Lowestoft Road, North Cove, Beccles NR34 7PH (01502 476601; www.thethreehorseshoesnorthcove. co.uk). Memorabilia of equine origin adorn the interior of this 17th-C hostelry which serves real ales and food *L and E (not Sun E)*. Garden, dog- and family-friendly. *Regular* live music. Traditional pub games and Wi-Fi. *Open daily 12.00-00.00.*

🍴✕ **2 The White Lion** White Lion Road, Wheatacre, Beccles NR34 0AT (01502 677388; www.wheatacre-whitelion.co.uk). Surrounded by grassland and mature trees, this attractive pub serves real ale and food *Mon-Fri L and E & Sat-Sun 12.00-21.00 (Sun 18.00)*. Garden, dog-friendly. *Regular* live music. Newspapers, real fires and Wi-Fi. Camping nearby. B&B. *Open 12.00-23.00.*

🍴✕ **3 The Swan Inn** Swan Lane, Barnby, Beccles NR34 7QF (01502 476646; www.thebarnbyswan. co.uk). Complete with children's play area, pizza oven and barbeque, this country pub serves real ale and food *Mon-Sat L and E & Sun 12.00-18.00*. Garden, family-friendly. Real fires. B&B. *Open daily 11.00-23.00.*

🍴✕ **4 The Waveney Inn** Waveney River Centre, Staithe Road, Burgh St Peter NR34 0BT (01502 677599; www.waveneyrivercentre.co.uk). Lively, focal point of the River Centre, serving food (including takeaways) *daily 08.00-10.00 & 18.00-21.00 (Sun 12.00)* and real ale. Garden, dog- and family-friendly. Traditional pub games and Wi-Fi. Camping and lodges. Shop selling basic provisions and gifts. Open daily 08.00-23.00.

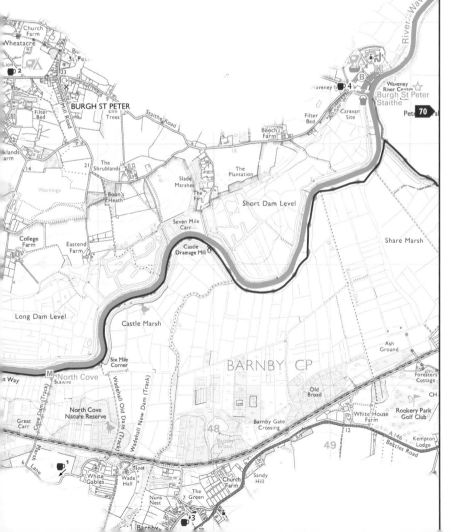

Oulton Broad

The Waveney continues its lonely course across the marshes. Oulton Dyke, an artificial channel, joins from the south: a link with Oulton Broad and the sea, via Mutford Lock.

● **Lowestoft**
Suffolk. All services. A town whose fortunes were made by the Dogger Bank and other North Sea fishing grounds in in mid-19th C. The arrival of the railway in 1847 brought the rich London markets within easy reach, thus putting the Thames estuary fishing ports out of business. By the turn of this century fishing had all but finished, and today the port has re-invented itself as a centre for renewable energy which is, in turn, displacing the port's previous affiliation with the oil and gas industries. The original fishing village was situated just north of Hamilton Dock and, although this is now an industrial estate, it is still possible to explore the Scores – narrow cobbled lanes which once led down to the herring curing houses of the old settlement.

With such a solid fishing heritage it is not surprising that the Lowestoft Lifeboat was founded as early as 1801, preceding the establishment of the Royal National Lifeboat Institute by 23 years. Of course, Lowestoft's alter ego is that of a popular East Coast resort, with excellent sandy beaches, two piers, plenty of parks and gardens, two theatres and all the usual seaside entertainments, extending both north and south of the harbour. At Lowestoft Ness one can stand at the most easterly place in England.

East Anglia Transport Museum Chapel Road, Carlton Coalville, Lowestoft NR33 8BL (01502 518459; www.eatm.org.uk). A museum of street transport, based around a recreated street scene of houses and shops, with vintage commercial vehicles, buses, trams and trolley buses, cars and a light railway. Visitors can take rides on different vehicles. Exhibition halls and *regular* special events. Picnic area, woodland walk, gift shop and tearooms. Well-behaved dogs welcome. *Opening times vary* so telephone or visit website for up to date information. Charge.

Lowestoft Lighthouse 3 Yarmouth Road, Lowestoft NR32 4AN (07709 836891; www. trinityhouse.co.uk/lighthouses-and-lightvessels/ lowestoft-lighthouse). The current lighthouse was built in 1874 (replacing an earlier structure dating from 1609) and stands 56ft tall and is 121ft above sea level. It cost £2,350 to construct. Its light can be seen from 26 miles out to sea and has been automated since 1975. Together with the two cottages used by the lighthouse keepers, it is a Grade II listed building.

Lowestoft Maritime Museum Sparrows Nest Park, Whapload Road, Lowestoft NR32 1UL (01502 561963; www.lowestoftmaritimemuseum. co.uk). Housed in an extended brick cottage, the museum charts the Town's history and seafaring and contains many large displays, models and artefacts. It also houses a variety of short video/ audio films on the history of the port of Lowestoft. Museum cinema and fascinating archive films.

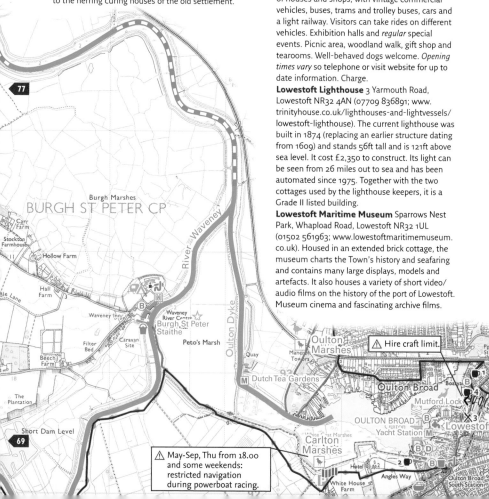

77

69

⚠ May-Sep, Thu from 18.00 and some weekends: restricted navigation during powerboat racing.

⚠ Hire craft limit.

Children's maritime identification trail. *Open daily 10.00-17.00. Last entry 16.00.* Charge.

Lydia Eva & Mincarlo Royal Plain, Lowestoft NR33 0AQ (01493 740760/07889 412333; www.lydiaevamincarlo.com) The *Lydia Eva* – the only coal-fired drifter in the world and the Mincarlo – the last sidewinder trawler – are floating maritime museums and now operated by a charitable trust. *Open daily 10.00-16.00.* Charge.

Pleasurewood Hills Family Theme Park Leisure Way, Lowestoft NR32 5DZ (01502 586000; www.pleasurewoodhills.co.uk). An award-winning theme park. Thrilling rides and white-water adventures, including the tallest rollercoaster in the east of England. Also shows, less demanding family rides and a miniature railway. Tearooms. *Opening times revolve around the school holidays so telephone or visit the website for details.*

Royal Navy Patrol Service Museum Europa Room, Sparrows Nest, Wapload Road, Lowestoft NR32 1XG (01502 586250, www.suffolkmuseums.org/museums/royal-naval-patrol-service-museum). At the outbreak of the Second World War Lowestoft became the Central Depot of the Royal Naval Patrol Service, with its HQ – HMS Europa – located in the Municipal Gardens known as the Sparrows Nest. The museum seeks to educate subsequent generations about this aspect of the War and, as the museum is housed in the former headquarters of the Royal Naval Patrol Service Association, there are always some ex-Patrol Service members available to provide a unique in-sight for visitors into the operations of the Patrol Service. *Open Mon, Wed & Fri 09.30-12.30.*

St Margaret's Church 147 Hollingsworth Road, Lowestoft NR32 4BW (01502 573046; www.stmargaretslowestoft.co.uk). A spacious building with an imposing tower of c1300 and much flushwork decoration. Lions and angels wait at the entrance to the south porch, which is rib-vaulted inside. Graceful arcades line the continuous nave and chancel. Admire the fine east window, together with the stained glass in the window to its right, done in 1819 by Robert Allen; he worked at the Lowestoft China Factory, which enjoyed a transient existence from 1756-1803. See also the medieval brasses of skeletons in shrouds.

● **Oulton Broad**
Suffolk. PO, stores, chemist, off-licence, takeaways, fish & chips, butcher, library, garage, stations. A continuation of Lowestoft but a resort in its own right. The Broad is one of the country's premier boating lakes covering 130 acres and navigable virtually throughout. Sailing, cruising, powerboat racing, windsurfing and rowing provide an ever changing spectacle. The handsome maltings in the north east corner have been nicely converted into dwellings. The quayside offers immediate access to Nicholas Everitt Park where there are tennis courts, a café, bowling greens and a children's play park. Alongside is the Harbour Master's Office and the Yacht Station. Oulton Regatta week is held *annually in late Aug.*

Carlton Marshes Nature Reserve Carlton Marshes Suffolk Wildlife Trust, Burnt Hill Lane, Carlton Colville, Lowestoft NR33 8HU (01502 359480; www.suffolkwildlifetrust.org/carlton). A pleasant walk along the public footpath to see marshland birds such as snipe, lapwing, bearded tits, ducks, geese, hobby and marsh harrier. An astounding 28 species of dragonfly have been spotted here. Trails, disabled access, shop, café, toilets and picnic area. *Open dawn to dusk.* Free.

Lowestoft Museum Broad House, Nicholas Everitt Park, Oulton Broad NR33 9JR (01502 511457; www.lowestoftmuseum.org). Housed in a 17th-C, Grade II listed building, the museum is home to an important collection of 18th C Lowestoft Porcelain; locally found fossils and artefacts and depictions of period room settings; local industry and people associated with the town, including Benjamin Brittain. *Open daily Apr-Oct 13.00-16.00.* Free.

Tourist Information Centre The Library, 92 Bridge Rd, Oulton Broad, Lowestoft NR32 3LR (01502 523442; www.eastsuffolk.gov.uk/contact-us/tourist-information). *Open Mon 10.00-16.00 & Tue-Fri 09.00-17.00 (Tue 09.30).*

NAVIGATIONAL NOTES

1 Tides: if you are making the passage through Great Yarmouth onto the Northern Broads you should aim to enter the Bure one hour after low water slack, thus avoiding any problems with low bridges.

2 Somerleyton Swing Bridge and St Olaves Bridge both have very low air draught at high water. *see* www.broads-authority.gov.uk/boating/navigating-the-broads/bridge-heights-and-opening-times.

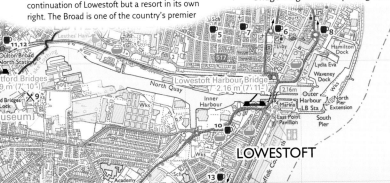

LOWESTOFT

Oulton Broad

▶✕ 1 The Commodore 15 Commodore Road, Oulton Broad, Lowestoft NR32 3NE (01502 508231; www.moss-co.com). A modernised traditional building, in an elevated position, with stunning views from the terraced garden over Oulton Broad. There is a good range of real ales, together with freshly cooked food available *Mon-Fri L and E & Sat-Sun 12.00-21.00 (Sun 18.00)* using local and seasonal ingredients. Garden, dog- and child-friendly. *Regular* live music. Wi-Fi. *Open 10.00-23.00 (Fri-Sat 01.00).*

▶✕ 2 The Quayside Bar & Restaurant Broadland Holiday Village, Marsh Road, Oulton Broad, Lowestoft NR32 9JY (01502 500895; www. broadlandvillage.co.uk). Situated in the middle of the holiday village, this child-friendly pub serves *real ale and food Tue-Fri L and E and Sat-Sun 12.00-21.00 (Sun 18.00)*. Terrace, dogs welcome outside. *Occasional* live music. Traditional pub games and Wi-Fi. B&B. *Open Tue-Thu L and E & Fri-Sun 11.30-23.00 (Sun19.00)*. Also caravans, lodges and bungalows for rent. Mooring.

✕♨ 3 The Red Herring Restaurant Bridge Road, Oulton Broad, Lowestoft NR33 9JT (01502 565666; www.redherringwinebar.com). Chinese restaurant situated in the old port area of Oulton Broad serving food *daily 16.00-23.00*. Mooring. Delivery service.

▶✕ 4 The Wherry Hotel Bridge Road, Oulton Broad, Lowestoft NR32 3LN (01502 516845; www.wherryhotel.com). Grand Victorian hotel overlooking the sea lock at the head of Oulton Broad serving real ale, full English breakfast and *all day* carvery *11.30-22.00*. Terrace, dog- and child-friendly. Wi-Fi. B&B. *Open 07.00-23.00.*

▶ 5 The Mariner's Rest 60-62 Rotterdam Road, Lowestoft NR32 2HA (01502 218077; www. facebook.com/themarinersrest). Deriving its name from proximity to the local cemetery, this welcoming community local serves real ales and real ciders. Garden, dog-friendly. Traditional pub games and sports TV. *Open Mon-Sat 11.00-00.00 & Sun 12.00-23.30.*

▶ 6 The Oak Tavern 71 & 73 Crown Street West, Lowestoft NR32 1SQ (01502 537246; www. facebook.com/theoaktavern). Featuring a bar festooned with Belgian brewery memorabilia, this popular community local serves real ale. Patio, dog-friendly. Traditional pub games and sports TV. *Open Mon-Sat 11.00-23.00 & Sun 12.00-21.30.*

▶ 7 The Stanford Arms 94 Stanford Street, Lowestoft NR32 2DD (01502 587444). A traditional pub, nicely refurbished, serving real ales and real cider. Courtyard seating, dogs welcome. Wi-Fi. *Open Mon-Thu 16.00-00.00; Fri 15.00-01.00 & Sat-Sun 12.00-00.00 (Sun 22.00).*

▶ 8 The Triangle Tavern Triangle Market Place, 29 St Peter's Street, Lowestoft NR32 1QA (01502 582711; www.green-jack.com). Purveyor of a wide range of the award-winning Green Jack Brewery's real ales – and reputed to be the country's most easterly brew pub – this lively town-centre tavern also dispenses real cider. Outside seating, dog- and family-friendly. *Friday* live music. Traditional pub games and sports TV. *Open Mon-Thu 11.00-23.00 (Thu 00.00) Fri-Sat 11.00-01.00 & Sun 12.00-22.30.*

✕♨ 9 The Third Crossing 6 School Road, Lowestoft NR33 9NW (01505 583596; www. thethirdcrossing.co.uk). Set in the picturesque Haven Marina on Oulton Broad, this friendly restaurant majors on seafood and steaks ... or you can just have a drink. Food sourced from local suppliers wherever possible. *Open Mon-Thu 09.30-14.30 and 17.00-20.00 & Fri-Sun 09.30-21.30 (Sun 15.00).*

▶✕ 10 The Spring Tide Kirkley Rise, Lowestoft NR33 0FD (01502 567898; www. springtidepublowestoft.co.uk). About a decade old, this newly-constructed pub serves real ale and food *daily 11.00-21.00*. Patio, family-friendly. *Open 11.00-23.00.*

▶ 11 The Ole Frank Pub Oulton Broad, Lowestoft NR32 3DQ (01502 512031; www.facebook.com/ olefrankph). Lively, modern estate pub, where the decoration is framed sports shirts, serving real ale. Outside seating, family-friendly. Traditional pub games and sports TV. *Open Mon-Sat 12.00-01.00 (Fri-Sat 02.30) & Sun 12.00-23.30.*

▶✕ 12 The Blue Boar 28 Oulton Street, Oulton, Lowestoft NR32 3BB (01502 585595). Former coaching inn and now a restaurant and bar serving real ale and food *Tue-Sat L and E and Sun 12.00-20.00*. Garden, dog- and child-friendly. *Open Sun-Mon 12.00-23.00 & Tue-Sat 11.00-23.00. Out of season open Tue-Sun L and E.*

▶✕ 13 The Oddfellows 6 Nightingale Road, Pakefield, Lowestoft NR33 7AU (01502 538415). A small, cosy, wood-panelled pub close to Pakefield's cliffs and the sea, dispensing real ale and food *L and E (not Sun E)*. Outside seating back and front, dog- and child-friendly. Sports TV and Wi-Fi. *Open Mon-Sat 11.00-23.00 & Sun 12.00-22.30.*

MOORINGS
Oulton Broad Yacht Station
Charges £5 for a short stay and £9.50-£24 overnight. Showers, toilets and laundry service available. 01502 574946.

St Olaves

Below the Railway Swing Bridge at Somerleyton the higher ground to the north east finally comes close to the river, the wooded Herringfleet Hills contrasting with the reed-fringed marshes that have typified the river since Beccles. At St Olaves the Haddiscoe New Cut leaves the river, providing a short cut to the River Yare and Norwich. Its course is very straight and quite dull, with only birds and the odd local train to provide interest. The river passes a hive of boating activity at St Olaves, with a fine old *pub* by the bridge, and Priory Mill a little further downstream. Then it is back into the marshes and the approach to Breydon Water. Along here it is a very different form of Broads boating from that experienced, say, at Hickling or Wroxham. Perhaps it is the tang of a salty breeze, suggesting the thrill of the sea.

NAVIGATIONAL NOTES

Tides: If you are making the passage through Great Yarmouth Harbour and onto the Northern Broads, you should aim to enter the Bure *one hour after low water slack*, thus avoiding any problems with strong tides and low bridges. If you are in any doubt check with the boatyards at St Olaves or Burgh Castle.

● **Somerleyton**
Suffolk. PO box, station. An irregular estate village, built by Sir Morton Peto and designed by John Thomas, who was also responsible for the Hall and the flint and stone church – a modern reproduction in the style of the local ecclesiastical architecture. To the north west is St Margaret's Herringfleet, a Norman structure, with a round tower and original Norman windows. The many and varied estate properties, particularly those grouped around the village green, have the makings of a model village. The villages' other claim to fame is as the home of the hovercraft.
Herringfleet Mill Three quarters of a mile west of the church and a unique survivor. This Grade II*, octagonal, three-storey timber-smock drainage windpump was built c1820 to a very early design, driving a 16ft diameter scoop wheel. It once had cloth sails, turned into the wind by a marshman who was expected to appear whatever the weather to perform this task. Indeed, a couch and a fireplace were provided so that he could attend the mill non-stop if required. It is preserved in full working order by Suffolk County Council and listed by Historic England at www.historicengland.org.uk/listing/the-list/list-entry/1183297.
Somerleyton Hall The home of Lord and Lady Somerleyton. A splendid and extravagant Victorian Mansion in mainly Jacobean style around a Tudor shell. It was built by John Thomas in 1846 for Sir Morton Peto, an extraordinarily successful man who began his career as a builder's apprentice and who, by the age of 31, was responsible for building Nelson's Column, St James's Theatre together with railways in the Argentine, Australia and Canada. Knighted in 1855, he was bankrupted in 1886 and the house was sold to Sir Francis Crossley. Liberal dressings of stone imported from Caen and Aubigny, superbly carved and restored at the end of the last century, adorn the brickwork. The splendid interiors contain paintings

by Landseer, Wright of Derby and Stanfield, with wood carving by Wilcox and Grinling Gibbons. In the 12 acres of garden, planted with azaleas and rhododendrons, is a maze dating from 1846 which is one of the finest in the country. The stable clock was the original model of a clock designed for the Houses of Parliament by Vulliamy in 1847. The glasshouses are by Paxton, designer of the Great Exhibition building of 1851. Miniature railway. *Open Apr-Sep: Hall and gardens open Tue, Thu, Sun & B Hols 10.00-17.00.* Garden only *open Wed.* Charge.

● **St Olaves**
Suffolk. Station (Haddiscoe). A pretty Broadland village, that over the years has made good use of the building stone from the dismantled priory to the north. The *PO and stores* are in Fritton, almost a mile east of St Olaves.
St Olaves Priory Beccles Road, St Olaves NR31 9HE (0370 333 1181; www.english-heritage.org.uk/visit/places/st-olaves-priory). The remains of a 14th-C Augustinian priory, beside the River Waveney, established around 1216. Following the Dissolution, under Henry VIII, the priory was owned by Sir Henry Jerringham who, in 1547, incorporated the remains of the monastic buildings into a new manor house on the site. However, little of this survived when the priory was dismantled in 1784. Around 1825 the floor of the refectory undercroft was raised and the building was converted into a cottage which was occupied until 1902. The hidden gem in this unassuming ruin is its 14th-C refectory undercroft. Its vaulted brick ceiling is an important early example of the use of brick in England. Supported on Purbeck marble columns, it is still almost complete and retains much of its original plasterwork. The only parts of the church to survive are a stretch of the south aisle, the west wall and parts of the north wall. The foundations of some of the brick-faced piers that supported the cloister arcade are visible, but nothing remains of the west range except the flintwork cloister wall, which is

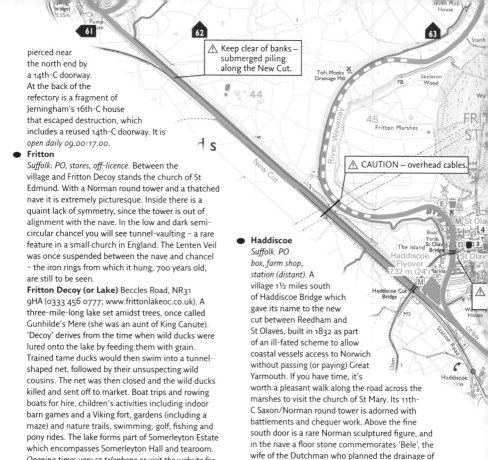

pierced near the north end by a 14th-C doorway. At the back of the refectory is a fragment of Jerningham's 16th-C house that escaped destruction, which includes a reused 14th-C doorway. It is open daily 09.00-17.00.

● **Fritton**
Suffolk. PO, stores, off-licence. Between the village and Fritton Decoy stands the church of St Edmund. With a Norman round tower and a thatched nave it is extremely picturesque. Inside there is a quaint lack of symmetry, since the tower is out of alignment with the nave. In the low and dark semi-circular chancel you will see tunnel-vaulting – a rare feature in a small church in England. The Lenten Veil was once suspended between the nave and chancel – the iron rings from which it hung, 700 years old, are still to be seen.

Fritton Decoy (or Lake) Beccles Road, NR31 9HA (0333 456 0777; www.frittonlakeoc.co.uk). A three-mile-long lake set amidst trees, once called Gunhilde's Mere (she was an aunt of King Canute). 'Decoy' derives from the time when wild ducks were lured onto the lake by feeding them with grain. Trained tame ducks would then swim into a tunnel-shaped net, followed by their unsuspecting wild cousins. The net was then closed and the wild ducks killed and sent off to market. Boat trips and rowing boats for hire, children's activities including indoor barn games and a Viking fort, gardens (including a maze) and nature trails, swimming, golf, fishing and pony rides. The lake forms part of Somerleyton Estate which encompasses Somerleyton Hall and tearoom. *Opening times vary so telephone or visit the website for details – similar to Somerleyton Hall.*

● **Haddiscoe**
Suffolk. PO box, farm shop, station (distant). A village 1½ miles south of Haddiscoe Bridge which gave its name to the new cut between Reedham and St Olaves, built in 1832 as part of an ill-fated scheme to allow coastal vessels access to Norwich without passing (or paying) Great Yarmouth. If you have time, it's worth a pleasant walk along the road across the marshes to visit the church of St Mary. Its 11th-C Saxon/Norman round tower is adorned with battlements and chequer work. Above the fine south door is a rare Norman sculptured figure, and in the nave a floor stone commemorates 'Bele', the wife of the Dutchman who planned the drainage of many of the marshes hereabouts.

FROM RIPPLE CRAFT TO HOVERCRAFT

Is it a boat? Is it a plane? Neither really, more like a hybrid of the two. That was how Christopher Cockerell's 1955 invention was initially perceived when he sought his first patent for the device he dubbed the 'Hovercraft'.

Born in 1910 to parents that were devotees of the Arts and Crafts movement – his father Sir Sydney Carlyle Cockerell was private secretary to Sir William Morris – Christopher elected to study engineering at Cambridge and upon graduation worked first for the Radio Research Company before joining Marconi in 1935. He went on to help develop radar and in the 15 years before he left, was named on 36 patents including the aerial direction finder and equipment used to pinpoint the locations of German radar stations on the northern coast of Europe.

In 1950 he took over a hire boatyard on the Broads at Somerleyton, which also produced the Ripple brand of cruisers and caravans. Clearly this did not fully occupy his fertile mind as he was soon thinking about heavy craft that could be supported on a cushion of air: the uncharitable suggesting that this would improve the performance of the somewhat ungainly Ripple cruiser range!

Shortly after Cockerell unveiled his working prototype in 1958, the National Research and Development Agency paid for a 'vehicle' based on his design to be built by Sanders-Roe and the SR-N1 went on to cross the English Channel towards the end of the following year. The first passenger carrying version was launched in 1962, built by Vickers and dubbed the VA-3.

Christopher Cockerell earned more than 50 patents as his invention was developed, working both independently and for Hovercraft Development, and was Knighted for his services to engineering in 1969. Seemingly, at something of a loose end again, he turned his attention to research directed towards turning the energy of sea waves into electricity. He died in 1999.

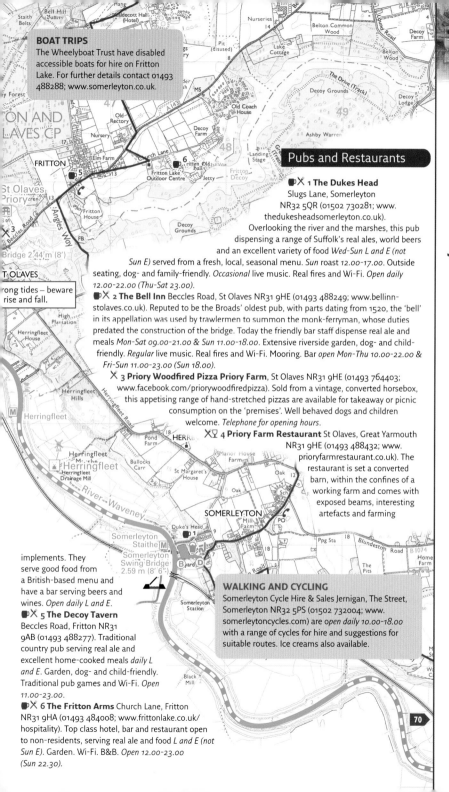

BOAT TRIPS
The Wheelyboat Trust have disabled accessible boats for hire on Fritton Lake. For further details contact 01493 488288; www.somerleyton.co.uk.

Pubs and Restaurants

1 The Dukes Head
Slugs Lane, Somerleyton NR32 5QR (01502 730281; www. thedukesheadsomerleyton.co.uk). Overlooking the river and the marshes, this pub dispensing a range of Suffolk's real ales, world beers and an excellent variety of food *Wed-Sun L and E (not Sun E)* served from a fresh, local, seasonal menu. *Sun roast 12.00-17.00.* Outside seating, dog- and family-friendly. *Occasional* live music. Real fires and Wi-Fi. *Open daily 12.00-22.00 (Thu-Sat 23.00).*

2 The Bell Inn Beccles Road, St Olaves NR31 9HE (01493 488249; www.bellinn-stolaves.co.uk). Reputed to be the Broads' oldest pub, with parts dating from 1520, the 'bell' in its appellation was used by trawlermen to summon the monk-ferryman, whose duties predated the construction of the bridge. Today the friendly bar staff dispense real ale and meals *Mon-Sat 09.00-21.00 & Sun 11.00-18.00.* Extensive riverside garden, dog- and child-friendly. *Regular* live music. Real fires and Wi-Fi. Mooring. Bar *open Mon-Thu 10.00-22.00 & Fri-Sun 11.00-23.00 (Sun 18.00).*

3 Priory Woodfired Pizza Priory Farm, St Olaves NR31 9HE (01493 764403; www.facebook.com/priorywoodfiredpizza). Sold from a vintage, converted horsebox, this appetising range of hand-stretched pizzas are available for takeaway or picnic consumption on the 'premises'. Well behaved dogs and children welcome. *Telephone for opening hours.*

4 Priory Farm Restaurant St Olaves, Great Yarmouth NR31 9HE (01493 488432; www. prioryfarmrestaurant.co.uk). The restaurant is set a converted barn, within the confines of a working farm and comes with exposed beams, interesting artefacts and farming implements. They serve good food from a British-based menu and have a bar serving beers and wines. *Open daily L and E.*

5 The Decoy Tavern
Beccles Road, Fritton NR31 9AB (01493 488277). Traditional country pub serving real ale and excellent home-cooked meals *daily L and E.* Garden, dog- and child-friendly. Traditional pub games and Wi-Fi. *Open 11.00-23.00.*

6 The Fritton Arms Church Lane, Fritton NR31 9HA (01493 484008; www.frittonlake.co.uk/ hospitality). Top class hotel, bar and restaurant open to non-residents, serving real ale and food *L and E (not Sun E)*. Garden. Wi-Fi. B&B. *Open 12.00-23.00 (Sun 22.30).*

WALKING AND CYCLING
Somerleyton Cycle Hire & Sales Jernigan, The Street, Somerleyton NR32 5PS (01502 732004; www. somerleytoncycles.com) are *open daily 10.00-18.00* with a range of cycles for hire and suggestions for suitable routes. Ice creams also available.

70

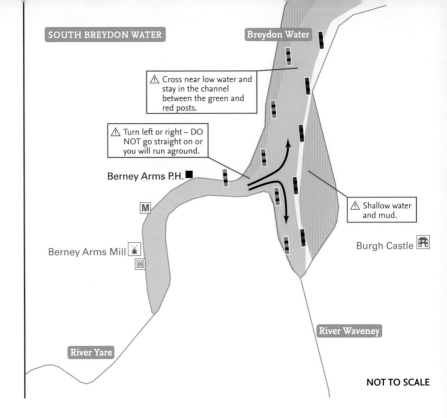

SOUTH BREYDON WATER

Breydon Water

⚠ Cross near low water and stay in the channel between the green and red posts.

⚠ Turn left or right – DO NOT go straight on or you will run aground.

Berney Arms P.H. ■

Ⓜ

⚠ Shallow water and mud.

Berney Arms Mill 🏛 Ⓜ

Burgh Castle 🏛

River Waveney

River Yare

NOT TO SCALE

GREAT YARMOUTH AND BREYDON WATER

You will have to pass through Great Yarmouth and across Breydon Water if you want to cruise between the northern rivers (Bure, Ant and Thurne) and the southern rivers (Yare, Chet and Waveney). This requires careful thought and forward planning. Additional information can be found at: www.broads-authority.gov. uk/boating/navigating-the-broads/getting-safely-through-great-yarmouth.

Breydon Water

(see South Breydon Water above)

- The Broads Authority operate a ranger patrol in the Breydon Water area.
- In high winds and at high tide, Breydon Water can be rough. Crossing at the right time, at low water, should avoid this problem.
- Everyone should wear a life-jacket when crossing Breydon Water.

- Do not navigate Breydon Water (or anywhere else) in fog.
- The Broads Authority have free 24 hour moorings between the Berney Arms pub and the wind pump (mill). Use them to wait for favourable tides to cross Breydon Water.
- For advice on whether or not to cross, contact your boatyard or telephone Broads Control on *01603 756056*.

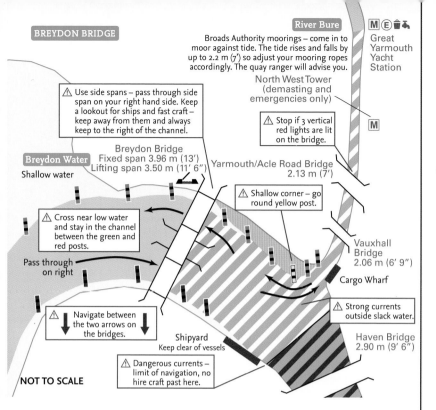

Great Yarmouth

(see Breydon Bridge above)

- You must time your arrival in Great Yarmouth to coincide with slack low water or just afterwards. Slack low water is around 1 hour after low water at Great Yarmouth Yacht Station. Check a tide table to find out when this is. At slack low water the current is weaker, so it is easier to moor, and there is more room under the bridges. At high water you will not be able to get under the bridges, and there is nowhere safe to moor to wait for the tide to drop on the Breydon Water side.
- It takes around 2¼ hours to travel from Acle to Great Yarmouth, and about 2 hours from Reedham or St Olaves. *See page 6 for journey times.*
- Check the map and follow the directions. The water is shallow outside the posted channel so it is important to keep within the posts.

- You may wait free of charge at Great Yarmouth Yacht Station while the tide drops to allow safe passage under the bridges.
- Always approach the moorings against the tide.
- It may be difficult to turn in the narrow river, so turn well upstream or down, depending on the tide, giving yourself plenty of time.
- If the river is busy, be prepared to go down through the bridges and turn where there is more room.
- You must not proceed downstream if three vertical red lights are on the Yarmouth/Acle Road Bridge.

Where to Hire

	Bicycle	Boat trips	Canoes	Electric boats	Motor boats	Rowing boats	Sailing dinghies	Learn to Sail (s)	Canoe (C) Windsurf (W) Padleboard (SUP)
Broads Tours (page 19) ♿ *The Bridge, Norwich Road, Wroxham, Norfolk NR12 8RX (01603 782207; www.broadstours.co.uk)*		✓		✓	✓				
Eastwood-Whelpton (page 27) *Upton Yacht Station, Upton, Norwich, Norfolk NR13 6BL (01493 750430; www.eastwood-whelpton.co.uk)*								✓	✓(S)
Ferry Marina (page 22) ♿ *Ferry Road, Horning, Norwich, Norfolk NR12 8PS (01692 631111; www.ferry-marina.co.uk)*					✓				
Richardson's Day Boat Hire (page 19) *Fineway Leisure, The Rhond, Hoveton NR12 8UE (01603 782309; www.richardsonsboatingholidays.co.uk)*				✓	✓				
Horstead Centre (page 18) *(Residential outdoor centre) Rectory Road, Horstead, Norwich, Norfolk NR12 7EP (01603 737215; www.horsteadcentre.org.uk)*									✓(C)
JB Boat Sales (page 22) *106 Lower Street, Horning, Norwich, Norfolk NR12 8PF (01692 631411; www.jbboats.co.uk)*					✓				
King Line Cottages & Day Boats (page 22) ♿ *Ferry Road, Horning, Norwich, Norfolk NR12 8PS (01692 630297; www.norfolk-broads.co.uk). Electric boat hire for the disabled & elderly.*				✓					
Mississippi River Boats (page 22) ♿ *The Swan Hotel, Lower Street, Horning, Norfolk NR12 8AA (01692 630262; www.southern-comfort.co.uk)*		✓							
Salhouse Broad (page 19) *Lower Street, Salhouse, Norwich, Norfolk NR13 6RX (01603 722775/07795 145475; www.salhousebroad.org.uk)*			✓						
Wherry Yacht Charter (page 19) *The Wherry Base, Barton House, Hartwell Road, Wroxham, Norfolk NR12 8TL (01603 781475; www.wherryyachtcharter.org)*									✓(S)

	Bicycle	Boat trips	Canoes	Electric boats	Motor boats	Rowing boats	Sailing dinghies	Learn to Sail (S) Canoe (C) Windsurf (W) Padleboard (SUP)
River Chet								
Pacific Cruisers (page 60) *Riverside, Pits Lane, Chedgrave, Loddon, Norfolk NR14 6NQ (01508 520321; www.pacificcruisers.co.uk)*				✓				
River Thurne								
Herbert Woods (page 48) *Bridge Road, Potter Heigham, Norfolk NR29 5JF (01692 670711/0800 144 4472; www.herbertwoods.co.uk)*		✓	✓	✓				
Hunter's Yard (page 48) *Horsefen Road, Ludham, Norfolk NR29 5QG (01692 678263; www.huntersyard.co.uk)*								✓(S)
Martham Boats (page 46) *Valley Works, Cess Road, Martham, Great Yarmouth, Norfolk NR29 4RF (01493 740249; www.marthamboats.com)*		✓		✓	✓	✓		✓(SUP)
Maycraft (page 48) *North West River Bank, Potter Heigham, Great Yarmouth, Norfolk NR29 5ND (01692 670241; www.maycraft.co.uk)*				✓				
Norfolk Broads School of Sailing (page 27) *Upton Yacht Station, Upton Acle NR13 6BL (01493 750430; www.norfolksailingschool.co.uk).*								✓(S)
Norfolk Wherry Trust (page 49) *Forsythe Wherry Yard, Horsefen Road, Ludham, Great Yarmouth, Norfolk NR29 5QG (www. wherryalbion.com).*								✓(S)
Phoenix Fleet Ltd (page 49) *Repps Staithe Boatyard, Bridge Road, Potter Heigham, Great Yarmouth, Norfolk NR29 5JQ (01692 670460; www.phoenixfleet.com)*		✓	✓	✓				
Whispering Reeds Boats Ltd (page 42) *Staithe Road, Hickling, Norwich, Norfolk NR12 0YW (01692 598314; www.whisperingreeds.net)*		✓		✓	✓	✓		

	Bicycle	Boat trips	Canoes	Electric boats	Motor boats	Rowing boats	Sailing dinghies	Learn to Sail (s) / Canoe (C) / Windsurf (W) / Padleboard (SUP)
River Waveney								
CC Marine (page 67) *Wherry Boatyard, 35 Northgate, Beccles,* *Suffolk NR34 9AU (01502 713703;* *www.ccmarinebeccles.co.uk)*					✓			
H E Hipperson (page 67) *Hipperson Boatyard, Gillingham Dam, Beccles, Suffolk* *NR34 0EB (01502 712166; www.hipppersons.co.uk)*				✓	✓			
Oulton Broad Dayboats (page 71) *6 Yacht Station, Bridge Road, Lowestoft,* *Suffolk, NR33 9JS (07933 662866;* *www.waveneyrivertours.com)*	✓				✓			
Outney Meadow Caravan Park (page 66) *Outney Meadow, Bungay, Suffolk NR35 1HG* *(01986 892338; www.outneymeadow.co.uk)*			✓					
Rowancraft (page 66) *Big Row, Geldeston, Beccles, Suffolk NR34 0LY* *(01508 518208; www.rowancraft.co.uk)*			✓	✓				
Waveney River Centre (page 67) *Sraithe Road, Burgh St Peter, Beccles, Suffolk* *NR34 0DE (01502 677343; www.waveneyrivercentre.* *co.uk)*			✓		✓	✓		
Waveney River Tours Ltd (page 70) ♿ *Mutford Lock Bridge Road, Oulton Broad,* *Lowestoft, Suffolk NR33 9JS (01502 574903;* *www.waveneyrivertours.com)*	✓				✓			
Waveney Sailability (page 70) ♿ *Excelsior House, Quay View Business Park, Barnards* *Way, Lowestoft, Suffolk NR32 2HD (01493 663837;* *www.waveneysailability.co.uk)*								✓(S)
Waveney Stardust (page 67) ♿ *Georgian House, 34 Thoroughfare, Halesworth, Beccles* *NR34 0EB (07817 920502; www.waveneystardust.* *co.uk). Boat suitable for the elderly and disabled.*	✓							
Whitlingham Great and Little Broads								
Whitlingham Outdoor Education Centre (page 54) *Whitlingham Lane, near Trowse,* *Norwich NR14 8TR (01603 632307;* *www.whitlinghamadventure.org.uk)*	✓		✓				✓	✓(SUP)

	Bicycle	Boat trips	Canoes	Electric boats	Motor boats	Rowing boats	Sailing dinghies	Learn to Sail (S) Canoe (C) Windsurf (W) Paddleboard (SUP)
Near the Rivers Bure and Thurne Clippesby Hall (page 27) *Clippesby, Norfolk NR29 3BL (01493 367800; www.clippesbyhall.com)*	✓							
Around the Norfolk Broads The Canoe Man provides canoe hire, training and guided canoe trails through the Broads. *Contact: 65 Bells Road, Gorleston, Great Yarmouth NR31 6AG (07873 748408; www.thecanoeman.com)*			✓					✓(C)
HOLIDAY HIRE **Boat booking agencies** Hoseasons Boating Holidays *Contact: Lowestoft, Suffolk NR32 2LW (01502 500505; 0345 498 6589; www.hoseasons.co.uk/boat-holidays/)*					✓			

♿ Wheelchair accessible – please contact the companies for further information.

Broads Authority Yacht Stations

Great Yarmouth Yacht Station (page 33) *Tar Works Road, Great Yarmouth, Norfolk NR30 1QX (01493 842794/07766 398238). Staffed Apr-Oct 08.00-20.00.* Moorings, help and advice.

Norwich Yacht Station (page 51) *Riverside Road, Norwich, Norfolk NR1 1SQ (01603 612980/07747 065378). Staffed Apr-Oct 08.00-20.00.* Moorings, pump out, help and advice.

Reedham Quay Riverside, Reedham (page 62) *Reedham, Norfolk NR13 3TX (01493 701867/ 07733 102566). Staffed Apr-Oct 09.00-18.00.* Moorings, help and advice.

For further details *see* www.broads-authority.gov.uk/ boating/facilities/yacht-stations.

There are also two local authority yacht stations – both offer moorings (charge):

Beccles Yacht Station The Quay, Beccles NR34 9BH (01502 712225/07938 845744; www. becclestowncouncil.gov.uk/the-town/beccles-quay-yacht-station).

Oulton Broad Yacht Station Bridge Road, Lowestoft NR33 9JS (01502 574946; www.yachtstation.co.uk).

NATURAL HISTORY

The total area of the Broads is 117 sq miles and is made up of 7 rivers and 63 Broads, most of which are less than 13ft deep. In the 12th C peat was used as an alternative fuel source to the diminishing timber supplies. Peat extraction was undertaken by hand and took place up to the 14th C when sea levels rose and water begin to seep into the pits forming the Broads you see today.

Today the wetlands of eastern England compromise one of the most fascinating regions of the British Isles, a world of open skies and wide vistas contrasting with dense reed beds and woodland. Although lacking the drama of mountains and rolling hills, this area provides in its rivers and marshlands the ideal habitat for numerous animal, bird and plant species. Those on boats are sure to see lapwing, cormorant, snipe, bittern and sandpiper (and even the common crane) using the water's edge; mallard, coot and moorhen on rivers and dikes; and great crested grebe and dabchick on the open water. Marsh harriers, kestrels and sparrowhawks soar above the countryside and the fortunate may catch a glimpse of the scarce Cetti's warbler. More ephemeral is the Norfolk harrier – a species of dragonfly – and the swallow-tail butterfly. While cruising gently through the 'unspoilt' countryside, it is easy to forget that these areas represent transitory, unstable habitats; much altered by man but also changing gradually as a result of natural processes.

The Broads offer a classic example of the impermanence of open-water sites. Most broads are between nine and twelve feet deep and were at one time rich with aquatic plants. Fringed with Norfolk reed or reed sweet grass in the tidal reaches, the reed-swamps encroach on the open water by the gradual accumulation of dead vegetation and the trapping of mud in root systems; on the landward side the swamp becomes drier and the land surface is gradually built up, to be colonised by other plants such as marsh pea, marsh fern and marsh orchid. These plants form the cover in which seedlings of alder and various willow species thrive, replacing the fen by a shrubby mixture of alder in the shallows, with oak, birch and ash in the drier areas. The alder *carr*, which is typical on the boundaries of the least disturbed broads, is the nearest thing in Britain to impenetrable jungle – a dense shrubbery growth, its roots hidden beneath the surface, all growing in a black glunitous mass which will bear your weight on one step but not the next. Perhaps it is because the reed-swamp, fen and carr are all so difficult for man to explore that they have become such a haven for wildlife.

Regrettably, in the 1950s and 1960s there was a deterioration in the water quality of many of the broads (and also in the reed-swamp areas, although for different reasons) which led to a decline in the plant and animal life. The major problem was one of water chemistry. An increase in plant nutrients – nitrates and phosphates derived from sewerage treatment works and leaching of chemical fertilisers from farmland – stimulated a massive growth of algae which had several detrimental effects. The water became turbid in summer – looking rather like thin pea soup – thus preventing the light penetrating more than an inch or so below the surface. The submerged water plants, once such a feature of the clear waters

Cetti's Warblers are not uncommon near the Broads

of the broads, were shaded out; without light they could not survive. This process is known as eutrophication.

An additional problem caused by the massive increase of algae is due to the fact that they precipitate calcium carbonate out of the water. This sinks, together with the great mass of dead algae generated each year, and the resultant build-up of soft mud means that virtually nothing except a small range of mud-dwelling, insect larvae can live on the bottom. Sedimentation in the sheltered, off-river broads, increased ten-fold at the rate of half an inch each year. In the relatively shallow waters of the broads this meant that it became impossible even to row across them; for animal life it was disastrous as virtually nothing could live in the oxygen-deficient water.

The first stage in reversing eutrophication in the Broads was to reduce phosphate input. Reducing nitrate input would have a similar effect but, due to the greater solubility of nitrates, this is harder to control. The discharge of treated sewage is recognised as the main source of phosphates in the waters of the broads. Iron compounds have been used to precipitate phosphates out of treated sewage in all nine treatment plants upstream of Barton Broad, initially cutting phosphorus levels in sewage discharge by 90%.

However, high levels of phosphate can remain present in the sediments at the bottom of waterways, preventing dissolved levels decreasing, even when the source is eliminated.

Suction dredging has been used across the Broads to both deepen waterways and remove the phosphate-rich sludge. Without stabilising the compacted peat beneath the sludge, it loosens and can release phosphorus at a similar rate. The growth of larger water plants, which stabilise the floor, is therefore necessary to complete the transformation.

Even with reduced nutrient levels, algae tend to remain dominant, blocking light and preventing plants from growing on the bed of the waterway. By manipulating the food chain – a process called biomanipulation – algae can be removed. To allow zooplankton to thrive, planktivorous fish have been largely removed from some Broads, normally by electrofishing. Around 75% of such fish must be removed for successful treatment. The explosion of zooplankton that results eats almost all algae, creating clear waters. Plants are then allowed to naturally recolonise the clearer waterways. The plant growth stabilises the floor, reducing the release of phosphorus. Their own nutrient uptake reduces the nutrients available to algae. Larger plants also create a favourable environment for predatory fish such as pike, which eat planktivorous fish, continuing to control their numbers. These effects eventually create a stable ecosystem where low growing, underwater plants dominate.

Elsewhere, management plans have been agreed with farmers to limit the amount of fertiliser used, as well as the type and quantity of pesticides, thus controlling the amount of pollutants leaching through the soil and into the water. In some broads, such as Barton, where recovery is well advanced, there have been extensive efforts made to restock with the native plants that were once so common.

Before Britain became an island in post-glacial times, its rivers were connected to those of mainland Europe and received elements of their rich flora and fauna. When the sea flooded the North Sea basin this connection was broken and those animals which depended on fresh water were trapped, being unable to disperse westwards into other rivers. This is particularly noticeable in the distribution of freshwater fish. Both the Broads and the Fenland rivers have more fish species than the rivers of western Britain and are distinguished by the presence of silver bream and ruffe (a relative of the perch). The Broads are famous for their pike, with fish of up to 40lbs being caught. Perch, bream and roach are also common.

The burbot, also known as eelpout and lingcod, was also found in these rivers at one time – the only member of the cod family to live in fresh water, it occurs eastwards across Europe, Central Asia and North America, but is now thought to be extinct in Britain; the last reported example occurring in the River Ouse system near Cambridge more than 50 years ago. However, plans are afoot to reintroduce this species – already a successful exercise in Germany and Belgium – and this is likely to happen in the very near future. The burbot will also be a beneficiary of recent beaver re-introductions as beavers are known to create burbot-friendly habitat.

The most exciting of all British insects, the swallow-tail butterfly, is a native of Broadland and is unique to the area – these insects are recognised as a distinct sub-species found only in this country. The first swallow-tails to emerge can be seen on sunny May days with their wings spread as they bask on reeds and sedges. During a fine summer they become more common, beating along the reed beds and occasionally flying inland high over alder carr as they mate. They lay their eggs on the milk parsley plant (another Broadland native) and, as they grow, become bright green with black and orange spotted rings on their bodies. They are hard to find, even when one knows where the correct plants grow, but are easy to identify once located. If alarmed, these larvae erect a bright orange horn just behind the head, which gives off a smell of pineapple.

The wildlife of the wetlands is still very rich, for while some species have declined, many others have increased. Typical of the reed beds is the bittern, a beautifully marked brown bird rather like a small heron in appearance. Although hard to spot, it can be recognised by its characteristic booming call. The reed beds also offer shelter to reed and sedge warblers and the grasshopper warbler's distinctive song can be heard by those who can distinguish it from the chirruping of a grasshopper or the ratchet on a fishing reel. Much rarer is Savi's warbler, which has a similar song. Other inhabitants of the reed beds are bearded tits and the marsh harrier, a large and rather uncommon bird of prey, which is gradually increasing its numbers on the Broads and nearby Fens.

By proceeding quietly, all these and more can be seen, a source of endless fascination for the naturalist and layman alike.

SAILING ON THE BROADS

No one will disagree that the best way to see the Broads is from the water – although there may be dispute about the best sort of boat to use. However, a sailing boat does seem so much more a part of the scenery than a boat with a diesel engine can ever be. Certainly, the ducks and other wildlife think so!

Don't be deterred if you haven't done much sailing. If you have a little experience – even in the smallest sailing dinghy – you will quickly learn to handle one of the sailing cruisers available for hire. If you have no experience at all, some of the boatyards offering sailing craft can provide short tuition session refresher training with an expert helmsman, well worth the relatively small extra charge. The waters of the Broads are an ideal area to learn to handle a large sailing boat. There is usually enough wind and seldom too much and, although the waters are tidal, there is no great rise and fall, neither are there waves of any size, so you can concentrate on the art of sailing without worrying about the problems of navigation or even sheer survival which are sometimes present at sea.

The boat hire companies issue detailed brochures from which you can select a boat with confidence – the boatyard entries in the guide on pages 80–86 list those with sailing craft for hire. The descriptions and specifications are usually accurate and it is worth noting that where they say 'suitable for yachtsmen with some experience' they mean someone who has sailed before – not necessarily Chay Blyth!

When you have committed yourself and confirmed the booking, you will be sent further literature with hints and tips. Read this carefully – all of it! The information is invariably well presented, certainly worth having, and can make the difference between a successful holiday and a disappointment.

Before you go to collect your boat, decide which of your party is the skipper (a piece of advice that applies to all boat hire and not just sailing boats). It doesn't matter if he or she isn't a Horatio Nelson – the important thing is that you can't sail a boat by committee.

The boatyard will explain the boat to you and organise any training you have booked. Make sure you pay attention and understand how everything works. Note how the boat is prepared for sailing so that you can reverse the process when you moor up at night.

This is not intended to be an instruction manual, but a few dos and don'ts might not be out of place:

1) Keep the boat tidy – this helps to avoid accidents and breaking crockery.
2) Hoist and lower sails only with the boat pointing into the wind.
3) Make sure you know how to lower and raise the mast.
4) Make sure you know how to reef sails. If it is very windy and you are apprehensive, then stay where you are until the wind drops a bit. There are no prizes for foolhardiness.
5) Don't try to sail into a leeward mooring. Lower sails head to wind first, and then motor or drift in to moor.
6) Try to help motor cruisers by signalling your intentions (if you're sure you know what they are).

THE NORFOLK WHERRY

The Norfolk Wherry was a trading craft that evolved to suit the particular conditions encountered on the Broads. Its precursor was the keel, a square-rigged sailing barge dating from the time of William the Conqueror. This type of rig made the craft difficult to sail in anything but a following wind and, together with the absence of paths from which to bank-haul, made for slow progress and frequent delays.

It was the Dutch who first introduced the fore and aft rig – the sort of rig we see on yachts today – to Britain during the 16th C, allowing craft to sail much closer to the wind (i.e. with the wind almost against the direction of travel) than had hitherto been possible.

The hull of the Norfolk Wherry has as its distant ancestor the passenger rowing boat, clinker-built, which was married to the new sail configuration giving a highly manoeuvrable craft which could operate under most conditions. The first such craft to be recorded was the *Spread Eagle*, constructed in the early 17th C. Gradually they were built larger and larger, culminating in the 40 tons to be found in the early 20th C. The original low-peaked gaff sail was eventually replaced by a high-peaked sail upon a long gaff, with the mast well forward. Even this mast was built to a special design. Unstayed, it pivoted at the top of the tabernacle and was counter-balanced by an enormous metal weight of up to two tons, which meant that it could be lowered quickly when passing under bridges, then raised again without the boat losing way. Crewed by a skipper and a mate (who may also have been his wife or mistress) the Norfolk Wherry had achieved the elegant simplicity of all good functional design.

Cargoes of virtually every description were carried and the wherryman knew every inch of the Broads they sailed on, using every trick in the book to reach their destinations. But, alas, with building of the railways and the roads, their days were numbered. By 1949 the last wherry had finally furled its sail and ceased trading. As usual, most were scrapped before their worth was realised and it was only the timely intervention of the (then) newly formed Norfolk Wherry Trust which saved the *Albion*. Although not wholly typical, being carvel-built, she is a wonderful reminder of bygone days. On most weekends during the summer, parties of enthusiasts are taken on sailing trips in this unique craft.

Subsequently, other wherries have been restored and are available for charter, details below:

Norfolk Wherry Trust Forsythe Wherry Yard, Horsfen Road, Ludham NR29 5QG (01508 580482; www.wherryalbion.com) **Wherry Maud Trust** La Rose, Pristow Green Lane, Tibenham NR16 1PU (www.wherrymaudtrust.org) and **Wherry Yacht Charter** The Wherry Base, Barton House, Hartwell Road, Wroxham NR12 8TL (01603 781474; www.wherryyachtcharter.org).

The Wherry Albion *near Horning*

INDEX